WON'T BE SILENT

DON'T STOP 'TIL IT MATTERS

WON'T BE SILENT

DON'T STOP 'TIL IT MATTERS

Embracing my superpowers of humor and optimism to survive being second-generation Holocaust, coming out, addiction, and endless unbelievable obstacles

Abe Gurko

NEW YORK ■ LOS ANGELES

Published by Won't Be Silent LLC
Hardcover: 979-8-9900053-2-7
Paperback: 979-8-9900053-1-0
Kindle: 979-8-9900053-3-4
Audiobook: 979-8-9900053-4-1

Library of Congress Control Number and Cataloging-in-Publication data on file with the publisher.

Cover design by Marc Balet
Cover Photo: Diana Gomez

Back Cover Photo: Rankin

Publishing and Production services by Concierge Marketing Inc.

Printed in the United States of America

10 9 8 7 6 5 4 3 2

*To my incredible sisters
Vivian and Rita,
who have seen me through thick and thin—
literally and figuratively.*

Contents

PREFACE

Hello, Gorgeous!

Welcome to the abridged version of my life. Since Alzheimer's runs in my family, I felt compelled to jot down (and am glad to have remembered) some of my life-changing stories and momentous occasions to share with you. Here are the pivotal stories that have propelled me to become the person I'm (finally) happy to be.

- To those of you who found your way here through my TikTok page expecting brutal honesty, some laughs, and a touch of MAGA bitch-slapping, you will get what you came for.
- To those of you who refused to join TikTok because Instagram tickles your fancy and the few musings that I post there interested you enough to come here, I have included several images so you will feel right at home.
- To those of you who wound up here through Facebook, I am happy to know that it still works.

The reason I wrote this book is to emphasize the importance of making your life matter. Mattering came late in the day for me as I had to overcome seemingly insurmountable challenges to get there. In hindsight, I would not change an iota since it all brought me to this point of self-love, gratitude, and appreciation for life. Hopefully, you will come away from *Won't Be Silent* shouting from the rooftops, "I laughed, I cried, it was better than *Cats*."

Love,

ABE

FOREWORD

The very idea of a foreword, as I ponder here—forces the person writing it (in this case, myself) to look backward. Walking backward into that soft pool of memory is meant to help set up or equip the reader for the journey ahead. To provide a foundation before the attending audience jumps faithfully into the dark. And while you may have relied on the security of that cool foundation in other books, I offer you instead—an invitation to experience this story a bit differently…because it is a different kind of story.

To me, Abe Gurko is not the simplest of men, so his story, naturally, is not a simple one. This book is an adventure, a labyrinth that winds to a path to self-discovery and subsequent acceptance. First, into that backward place that helps to explain how Abe, the person, came to be… and then as a witness, into the satisfying anticipation of a reignited star, whose brilliant, unexpected arrival brings light pulsing with newfound purpose.

For me, reading these pages unlocked emotions of every kind. I found myself wiping away long-forgotten tears at some points while giggling happily through many other hilarious situations and wild revelations. Abe's accounting here is complex, unpredictable, and profoundly truthful. And while he was dealt challenges that would have broken a lesser spirit—his is an unyielding, unapologetic commitment to persevere.

Now, I have had the benefit of over two decades of friendship, getting a front-row seat to Abe's life and some of what you're about to experience, but even now, I sit here, awestruck, grateful, and in complete admiration of my friend. His acerbic wit, so characteristic of his natural sensibility, is not cynical but a deft and precise way of dealing with the world around him...and the very refusal of silence (as the title offers) is a summoning for all of us. Even when life seemed intent on muzzling him, smashing his opinions, quieting his rage, heartbreak, or joy—he kept going.

If you understand the reference, Abe is the Laverne to my Shirley, a punchy, reliable co-star in a yet-to-be-filmed TV comedy. Together, we've made the art of celebrating even the smallest victories with the loudest, heart-affirming fits of laughter. We've also navigated some of life's bigger disappointments, in mutual agreement that almost everyone else (but ourselves, of course) is annoying and, much to my chagrin, that he is somehow always right... about everything.

And so, it's with a great measure of pride that after years of encouragement, eagerly anticipating the moment that this book would come into being, I have the honor of leading you into the pages of this momentous dance—a vulnerable collection of threads, written in the unique, immutable voice of my friend Abe.

So, buckle up, dear reader... this story will twist, turn, and bend into unexpected places—but while exploring the labyrinth—may you find inspiration, laughter—and, above all else, the undeniable realization that when life pressures you into silence, you too have the power to defy it and make your story heard.

—Stephen Galloway

"Our lives begin to end the day we become silent about things that matter."

— Martin Luther King Jr.

INTRODUCTION

t wasn't until my teens that I realized how awkward it was to say that New Jersey was my home state. The year was 1973; I was short, fat, and four-eyed with no immediate hopes of having a life worth living. At bittersweet sixteen, all I aspired to be was someone else. Preferably someone famous. By no means was I a candidate for becoming a jet-setter, and I had no foreseeable prospects of hobnobbing in the South of France with the lanky Mick Jagger, the groovy Penelope Tree, or the beautiful, haunting Marianne Faithfull. Nope. Not from my barely upper-middle-class situation, far from that madding crowd.

Sadly, fate had me nestled atop the Palisades in a perfectly mani-cured suburban hamlet just north of the George Washington Bridge, a mere hop, skip, and light-year away from the fierce, pulsating beat of Manhattan. So close, yet so far. Somehow, the modest, red brick, split-level affair I called home didn't have the same *joie de vivre*. Our house was heavier on *vivre* and lighter on *joie*. At a young age, I realized I was different from everyone else, which made me want to be someone else! Someone who was taller, blonder, didn't need glasses, not Jewish, defi-nitely thinner, perhaps most notably from somewhere else. Looking the way I did, I was afraid of becoming the neighborhood joke. Only it wouldn't be funny. I needed to become someone of note and find purpose. And above all, to matter. The game was afoot.

My mother, Henny, a diminutive, fiery, delusional woman, was hell-bent on creating the illusion of royalty. Having survived the concentration camps during World War II, she was determined to live in an environment that reeked of opulence, even if it was the last thing she did. It was her way of thumbing her nose at the Nazis. Picture this: our French provincial living room had grass-green shag carpeting, a mint-green velvet Empress Josephine couch, and red crushed velvet Louis XVI conversation chairs. Accessorize that with lamps that were life-size statues of naked women adorned with teardrop crystals and a Grecian pillar topped with the bust of Venus de Milo, just kind of sitting there. My mother's dreck-orator (as she lovingly called Mr. Chasen) had selected mint-green, flocked wallpaper covered with art (using the term loosely) that highlighted my mother's prized collection of Morris Katz toilet paper art originals. (Katz was a Holocaust survivor who drove around the Catskills every summer, showing up at various bungalow colonies unannounced to much fanfare.) Mr. Chasen finished the look with dramatic window treatments that were exact replicas of the green curtains from Tara—the ones Scarlett O'Hara had Mammy stitch up to scam Rhett Butler. My mother loved *Gone with the Wind*. My eldest sister's name is Vivian. Coincidence? I don't think so.

Our house was a kaleidoscope of colors; each room had a palette that would even upset the color-blind. Our kitchen counters were aquamarine; the wallpaper was a royal-blue-and-white floral pattern. My sister Rita's room was canary yellow with kelly-green plaid curtains and lime-green shag carpeting. My room was burnt orange with chocolate-brown and blue accessories. I decorated my walls with posters memorializing my favorite Academy-Award®-winning films. My father bought me a barbell that I rolled under the bed to keep out of sight, whereas my mom bought me a guitar since my piano skills weren't living up to her expectations. My parents' bedroom featured hot-pink walls, royal-blue carpeting, burgundy, pink, and white dramatic drapes, and pink crystal chandeliers flanking their bed, with a ceiling-high headboard covered in hot-pink-and-white toile fabric reminiscent of Marie Antoinette at Versailles. Are you sensing the not-quite-resplendent theme? No doubt the many frenetic, over-the-top color schemes influenced my ever-evolving psyche.

My mom, the glamourpuss

My mother's penchant for visuals and theatrics rubbed off on me. Since childhood, I've been obsessed with movies and movie stars from black-and-white melodramas, MGM musicals, screwball comedies, and classic horror films. I consumed them while stuffing my face with Dolly Madison ice cream and countless Caravelle bars. I lay in bed, covers pulled up to my second chin, surrounded by empty candy wrappers, watching *The Late Show* as well as *The Late, Late*

Show, enamored with the unattainable Hollywood dream machine, all the while worrying that there would never be a place in the sun for someone like me in that glorious, celluloid world. No, people like me watched from the sidelines as the parade passed by. It seemed like the closest thing to a brass ring that I would ever grab was an Entenmann's chocolate doughnut.

I retreated into the seemingly perfect celluloid world and watched countless movies at every chance. I loved the movies. I lived in the movies. I lost myself in the movies. The movies were a great place for a fat boy from New Jersey to escape. You could be anywhere, do anything, love anyone, and even kill someone. Heaven. *Gone with the Wind* and *West Side Story* sparked my obsession with Hollywood. There could have been no better entrée into the world of make-believe.

But a miracle occurred in the early 1970s. Suddenly, what had seemed hopeless and out of reach appeared on the horizon. That miracle occurred when Woody Allen's films became part of the American film vernacular. Vivian and I would run to the Baronet-Coronet Theater in New York City across from Bloomingdale's, where Woody Allen's movies always played. I was awed to realize that you no longer needed to look like Paul Newman or the Marlboro Man to get ahead in show business. Not with Woody Allen and Dustin Hoffman impacting the movie business. Ugly had become the new black.

Yet, I will never forgive Woody Allen for something that he did to me, personally, as a resident of New Jersey. His early films *Sleeper, Play It Again Sam,* and *Everything You Wanted to Know About Sex* were brilliant; however, they all contained condescending (and yes, perhaps humorous) references to my home state. These scathing digs made audiences howl with laughter, and at the same time, he ingrained into pop culture the notion that people from "Joisey" were at a disadvantage. Sitting in the dark, sold-out movie theater, I would slink down deep into the uncomfortable seat, covering my head with the giant tub of extra buttered popcorn as though a flashing neon arrow had identified me as the lone, lowly resident from that sad little state.

Because of Woody Allen, I wanted to stay in NYC forever and never go back to New Jersey. How was I ever going to become a member of the fabulii? That was my conundrum. I knew that I would probably have to create a false persona: someone who lived in Carnegie Hill, attended the Dalton School, and summered on the northern coast of Maine. You see, only the fabulii are allowed to use the word *summer* as a verb. I couldn't do that, and what, say "We summered in the Catskills"? That sounds like an oxymoron because it's the Borscht Belt where Jews would escape to beat the heat of the congested city, establishing clusters of Jewish ghettos, sans pogroms. Ghetto by choice, and I don't mean in a Missy Elliot kind of way.

What bothered me most was that Woody was just like me—a short, unattractive Jewish guy with gargantuan insecurities, though, frankly, his issues seemed more significant than mine. To make matters worse, he was from Brooklyn. In the '70s, the boroughs other than Manhattan were nowhere you wanted to be from because you'd be called a B&T (bridge and tunnel), a derogatory slam for people who lived outside of Manhattan. Admitting that you had to take a bridge or a tunnel to get to the city was so déclassé. B&Ts came from Brooklyn, Queens, the Bronx, and I guess, Staten Island, though I don't think that borough really exists. Staten Island is like Montana in the way that we see it on the map but no one's ever really been there. Seriously, have you ever slept with anyone from either of those places? I rest my case. I'll admit people from New Jersey were also considered B&Ts, but that's beside the point.

So, you can see the quandary; my dilemma was prescient. What could I possibly accomplish that would make up for my shortcomings, literally and figuratively? Who doesn't want to achieve a modicum of success in life? Something good had to come out of my gift of gab; that much was clear. I needed to generate some kind of goodwill, something that would bring joy and laughter to people. A legacy of sorts. The tragedy that my parents had endured made it hard for me to imagine what I could possibly achieve one day. I couldn't emulate that, nor even try to. So, I had to come up with some kind of plan to make them—or at least myself—proud. I was damned if I wasn't going to matter somehow, some way. I was determined to find a way to wiggle my five-foot-by-five-foot frame into the ever-exploding pop culture revolution that people like Woody Allen were enjoying. My journey to mattering had begun. Off to see the wizard I went.

HUMBLE BEGINNINGS

y story begins in the wee little town of Weehawken, which I lovingly refer to as "the welcome mat of New Jersey." Weehawken is twenty blocks long and three blocks wide, situated on the ass-end of the Lincoln Tunnel. Its only redeeming quality was that it overlooked the Manhattan skyline. Looking at the panoramic landscape of city lights from across the way in the *shtetl* I called home, I realized at a young age that I belonged on the other side of the Hudson River, the right side. Weehawken's claim to fame, if you can call it that, was its historic dueling grounds, where in 1804, sitting Vice President Aaron Burr killed General Alexander Hamilton. A bust of Hamilton stands at that site and tells the shocking story of the famous duel: an early teachable moment that even during the Revolutionary War, New Jersey was the perfect place to die. I had no interest in gaining notoriety through any means of violence, because with my luck, I'd be the one who met the fate of Alexander Hamilton—the dead guy.

Weehawken was your typical hideous, blue-collar town filled with anti-Semites and boozehounds, in that order. Our beyond-modest home was on a low-income, non-tree-lined street amid a glut of row houses. Think of the East End of London without the cachet of, well, London. Some would say these were humble beginnings, but that would be a step up to Highwood Avenue. The worst part of this scenario was its impact on my Holocaust survivor parents. They had come to America in search of streets paved with gold, only to stumble upon the completely downtrodden opposite. They had made a wrong turn somewhere between Ellis Island and Hester Street.

The Gurko family was close-knit, its weave woven so tightly that we sometimes couldn't untangle or breathe. I was the youngest of three, with two older sisters, Vivian and Rita. Our home was always filled with laughter in spite of our parents' past. We gathered nightly around the kitchen table as my mother, a phenomenal cook and baker, whipped up mouthwatering Eastern European dishes, cakes, and cookies. We loved keeping her company as the aroma of simmering pots filled with deliciousness kept us seated in anticipation. My mother was quick-witted, which rubbed off on us all, creating a giddy atmosphere. What went on inside our home was vastly different from what happened in the streets of Weehawken.

We were just about the only family of Jews in that shithole of a town. Most Jewish immigrants had settled in Brooklyn or the Lower East Side of Manhattan. Fate led my dad to get a job selling rags to gas stations in New Jersey, so off we went to the wrong side of the world. Imagine surviving Dachau and a Siberian work camp, only to end up in an oppressive environment where non-Jewish kids chased your children from their yellow parochial school bus. I don't know what's scarier, Nazis or blue-collar Joiseyites. The only real difference is the accent. And the latter can be just as off-putting as German. Neither are Romance languages.

My mother talked about what had happened to her family as far back as I can remember. She would tear up when speaking about her gifted musician brother, Wolf, who was killed in a concentration camp. She talked about how her parents were taken to the Ponary Forest and shot along with all the older Jews. She described the horrendous conditions when they were forced to live in the Vilna Ghetto with thirty people sharing a one-bedroom apartment. My mother's willingness to talk about her painful experiences and the cruelty she had witnessed taught us invaluable lessons about the world. She wanted us to know about the existence of pain and suffering, not only hers but that of the Jewish people, thus planting the seed of awareness that would eventually compel me to understand and embrace the importance of speaking up and sharing our stories, no matter what.

Until I was five years old, all the kids in our neighborhood accepted me. Everything changed the first time I got off the bus from a private Yeshiva I attended instead of a public school. The little Jew-haters in my neighborhood saw me get off a busload of Heebs wearing skull caps and ridiculed me. In hindsight, it was the first time in my life that I felt "other." I remember looking in the mirror and not liking what I saw. It was the beginning of wanting to be someone else. It was a reality check that left me hating people. I hated Jews for being Jewish, saddled with a stigma I might never break, especially because I was also fat, four-eyed, and short. I hated non-Jews for hating Jews. I began to lose faith in my faith and trust in my fellow man, questioning God's role in these unfortunate circumstances. The one saving grace of humanity were the actors and actresses on our RCA Victor black-and-white 10-inch TV screen—my refuge where I could escape and become someone else. Something had to change regarding the sad state of my reality.

Dear God,
Of all the options on who and what one can be on Earth, are
you sure this is what you really want for me? Is this perhaps a
mistake, and something you can correct? I'm ready to share a
few better ideas for a happy life. I'll wait.
Please advise.
Peace,
ABE

Aside from the stigma of other-ness, things at the Gurko house were fairly normal. Happy even. I looked up to my parents like they were superstars. They were my Liz and Dick but without booze, money, and celebrity status. I looked at my parents through rose-colored glasses. It wasn't until years later that I realized they weren't celebrities at all. They were two lovely people trying to live their best lives, having suffered the unimaginable. They were relegated to hustling my sisters and me around to rickety bungalow colonies in the Catskill Mountains in the sweltering summertime, sipping Manischewitz Concord Grape Wine and the occasional snifter of Slivovitz, the other Jewish alcohol.

My mother was a coloratura soprano in her youth before her career was cut short. At 18, she was en route to her first solo radio performance in Vilna, being the first "Jewess" to sing "Ave Maria" publicly. It was October 1941; she witnessed mass confusion in the streets, people running, screaming, mothers grabbing their children, personal belongings being hoisted onto wagons, and an overall atmosphere of impending doom. The Russians had invaded Poland. Hence, Henny's moment of glory was stolen, along with her innocence and, shortly thereafter, her dignity. That life-changing day and the denial of that accomplishment stayed with her until she took her last breath.

It was crucial to my mother that at least one of her children became a singer. She would take each of us, one by one, into her shocking-pink bedroom and announce, "Let's see if you have hidden talent." My sister Vivian would jokingly ask Rita and me, "So, do you have H.T.?"

My mother needed to know whether or not we had any vocal skills worth cultivating.

She secretly hoped that one of us would live the life she never could. Instead, she lived vicariously through us. Every once in a while, she would emerge from the dark reality of what she'd been deprived of to test our musical acumen. When it was my turn to take the H.T. Challenge, sheepishly I entered her hot-pink sanctuary, unsure of myself or what song to sing, strategically settling on something from *West Side Story*. She loved that movie and had an affinity for Leonard Bernstein, who had accompanied her in a post-war concert in Germany during the Nuremberg Trials, the high point of the short career that she was ultimately deprived of.

My mother being accompanied by Leonard Bernstein

in Munich, 1948

"Okay, now, sing," she instructed.

Deep breath in.

"I feel pretty, oh so pretty,

I feel pretty and witty and gay.

And I pity any girl, um, boy who isn't me today."

Not that I felt pretty, witty, or gay…at least not yet. I did have a good voice, but my overall package didn't stand a chance at stardom. Mom wouldn't dare say a word about my appearance. She loved me too much to criticize the Pillsbury Dough Boy look I was sporting.

See what I mean?

APRIL FOOL

1968 was such a volatile year, between the heart-breaking tragedies of Martin Luther King's and Bobby Kennedy's assassinations at the hands of madmen and body counts from the raging Vietnam War. College students were protesting warmongers, and Hippies were still tweaking on acid from the Summer of Love. But nothing was as intense as the critical, life-changing moment when—at the tender age of eleven—I had to start attending a new school on April 1st of that turbulent year.

We had recently "moved on up" from the dregs of Weehawken to the upper-middle-class hamlet of Englewood Cliffs, far from the Yeshiva of Hudson County where I was miserable. The horrific reality that I would have to change schools in the middle of a semester created high anxiety. Chubby people don't like drawing attention to themselves, and I was being hurled into a whole new world on—of all days—April Fools' Day. I cannot overstate the gravity of that reality.

"I don't want to go."

"You're going," my mother said sternly, having just polished my black penny loafers.

"Here." She forced my black-and-white checked blazer on my arms and handed me a crisscross tie to finish the look.

"They're going to love you. Everyone loves you. I love you."

Cringe.

She had no clue as to the level of dread I was experiencing at the prospect of having to walk into a new environment alone and fat. Yet another example of my fears falling on deaf ears because once you've survived a concentration camp, nothing else comes close. We walked up the street in silence and entered the main office, where heads turned as if they heard my heart pounding in my chest. I looked out to the hallway and noticed a few kids wearing jeans and sneakers.

"That's odd," I thought.

The mandatory dress code at the Yeshiva was a white tailored shirt, tie, jacket, proper slacks, and shoes—no sneakers. Who knew that kids in the suburbs went to school wearing street clothes? Jeans, T-shirts, sneakers. Boy, was I overdressed. Panic set in. The principal, a stocky Mr. Peterson, came out to greet us, and we followed him into his sterile office. The desk held mountains of manila folders, a large round Rolodex file, and a family photo. Middle America, here we are. Upper Middle, anyway. After a few niceties, my mother left me there. Mr. Peterson's assistant, a short, frizzy-haired woman dressed like a Tupperware Lady in a burnt orange, triple-knit, polyester pantsuit, walked me through a seafoam-green tiled hallway with a gray-speckled linoleum floor. Next stop: emotional breakdown.

Yikes.

I arrived at a faux wooden door with a narrow vertical window that gave me a glimpse into my immediate future. I took a deep breath as the Tupperware Lady swung the door open and we became the focus of attention for sixty adorable sixth-graders sitting in an unconventional square arrangement of desks. There would be no hiding behind Larry Bortniker as I had done at Yeshiva. I sensed that being the class clown as I had been at my last school could be helpful here and now. "Breathe," I told myself *sotto voce.*

Barely dipping a toe into the brightly lit room, I froze, as did the sixty students clad in an array of Easter-egg-colored shirts. Their faces looked confused, as though they'd seen the ghost of Christmas past or, in this case, a chubby nerd dressed for church. You could have heard a pin drop for what seemed like an eternity. The silence ended with one of the kids snickering on the left side of the room. I scanned the faces to identify the jerk who thought this monstrous moment was funny. I also tried not to make eye contact with anyone as my stomach began to churn. On the right side of the room there was another muffled snort by some other insensitive jerk. God forbid that the whole room exploded into laughter. That would have given me no choice but to activate my desperately needed, latent superpower and zap these motherfuckers, one by one, get arrested, charged, and sent to jail for the rest of my life. Prison suddenly sounded like a better option than being stuck in a room with this group of horrible, entitled, suburban brats. Eyes closed, I saw my life flashing by, and sadly, it wasn't interesting.

Two pretty women in their early thirties rushed to my side and introduced themselves as the "team teachers," part of an experimental concept. Unlike the traditional classroom structure I was used to, Group Dynamic Theory was the suburban rage. Miss Shevlin and Miss Jackson were well-dressed, spirited, single women. These teachers were a refreshing change from the disheveled, paunchy, Conservative rabbis in wrinkled black suits with *tzitzit* hanging out who taught Hebrew in the morning, while decrepit battleaxes taught English and math in the afternoons. Spending eight hours a day in an environment where I felt so out of place was partly to blame for my becoming an assimilated Jew. My negative attitude was intensified by having parents who gave me nightmares about what they had lived through during the Holocaust.

Under no circumstances did I want to take one step further into Dante's Inferno. I had to think fast on my feet in my shiny, black, penny-loafer shoes that I noticed a few kids staring at. I needed to change the dynamic in the room, keep my cool, act like nothing was afoot, and show these juvenile delinquents who's boss. Miss Jackson flashed a lovely smile and approached me. I quietly asked for permission to use the restroom, which was across the hall. I excused myself, went to the Boys' Room, looked in the mirror, and said, "What the fuck? What am I gonna do now?" I splashed cold water on my face, which was beet red from embarrassment, ripped off that blazer, tore off the stupid crisscross tie, untucked my shirt, unbuttoned the collar, rolled up both sleeves, took a last look at myself, gave myself a wink, walked back to the classroom, swung the door open with my garments rolled up in a ball, head held high, chest slightly puffed up, smiling as I announced, "Okay, I'm ready, where do I sit?"

Miss Jackson motioned me to sit down next to her. "This is your seat," she said with a reassuring wink and smile. She was the first black woman I had ever had the pleasure of meeting. This was also the first time I was surrounded by a group of kids my age who weren't exclusively Jewish, and the second time I had felt like an "other." Miss Jackson and I connected immediately; perhaps she felt like an "other" here in this room as well. I shoved the balled-up jacket and tie under my seat, sat down, smiled at her, turned to the class, and repeated, "Okay, I'm ready." The class chuckled, only they were not laughing at me but rather with me. Note to self: Crisis averted. Following my instincts had paid off in a way that would become a superpower at moments when the chips were down.

When I was in the seventh grade, The Moratorium to End the Vietnam War in Washington happened on November 15, 1969. America's youth culture at that time was deeply politically engaged and committed to ending the war. A wave of solidarity swept the nation as high school and college students boycotted classes because innocent young men were getting drafted into the army for what seemed like a senseless war. Our brothers, boyfriends, uncles, and cousins were coming back from Vietnam in body bags from a conflict that no one believed in. The song "War—What Is It Good For? Absolutely Nothing" was our anthem. Vivian was in college and participated in the Moratorium March with thousands of Hippies and peaceniks. I was proud to be related to an insurgent, so I spontaneously rallied my sixth-, seventh-, and eighth-grade classmates to stand with me in solidarity to boycott entering the school building. Acting like a community organizer, I chanted, "Give Peace a Chance" and rallied my classmates. Chaos ensued as students who had already entered the school came rushing out to join the cause. We had all been affected by looking at the black-and-white images from the front lines in Vietnam and the scrolling list of casualties on the 10 O'clock News.

This life-changing moment would be my first taste of activism, and it was delicious. It felt like we were on the cusp of changing the world. The Englewood Cliffs Police showed up within minutes because, outside of getting coffee and donuts, there was nothing for them to do in our tiny, manicured town chock-full of bleeding-heart liberals. The cops started ushering the kids back into the school, which infuriated me. In an act of rebellion, instead of heading back into the school, I ran toward the football field, which abutted a small patch of woods. As I ran, a feeling washed over me like I was escaping the Nazis, but let's face it, there was no comparison.

Running to the far end of the football field, I noticed another person—a girl— scurrying toward me. We veered into the woods and stood next to one another, breathless. By far, she was the prettiest girl in the school. Jessie was beautiful, and the way we met would foreshadow how, years later, she would become a consequential person in my life. We were the last holdouts of the anti-war protest, on the lam like Bonnie and Clyde. As I motioned her to follow me and hide behind a group of bushes, Jessie slipped on a wet pile of leaves and fell backward. I ran to her, cradling her head in my arms. We locked eyes, and I gazed into those piercing green eyes that would one day sashay with me into Studio 54.

She smiled, "I'm Jessie. You think we're gonna get suspended?"

Looking at that face, I froze, gently stroked her forehead, separating her overgrown bangs, and mustered the slightest grin, whispering, "Who cares? Let's lay low for a while." I hoped that "while" would last forever. "Are you okay?" I asked, slowly helping her up.

"I guess. What are we going to do now?" she wondered aloud.

"We are going to be proud of what we did today, and we'll go back and take the heat," I said, having fallen madly in love for the first time in my life.

We returned to the school followed by two Englewood Cliffs police officers who waddled their way across the field to retrieve us. After we had been escorted into the principal's office, our parents got involved. It was all over. Jessie's parents decided that this transgression was a clear sign that she needed a more disciplined environment, and the next day they packed her up and sent her off to boarding school. Even though we lived in the same hometown, I never got Jessie's phone number, so there was no chance to cultivate a friendship.

Maybe one day our paths would cross again, but I wasn't going to hold my breath for the unattainable. Based on experience, there wasn't a chance in hell that a romance between Jessie and me would ever see the light of day. In hindsight, Jessie was to me what Winnie Cooper was to Kevin Arnold from *The Wonder Years*. Besides, fat boys like me never got the girl. They befriended the girl, became the girl's confidante, and advised in matters of the heart. Having two sisters, I was happy to offer fashion and beauty tips and usually got to dance with the girls at house parties.

SIDEBAR: When a girl describes a boy as "a great dancer," you know that the overall package leaves much to be desired.

On a lighter note, in true Gurko fashion, I survived and thrived in middle school. I was voted Best All-Round Personality and Sunniest Disposition in the yearbook, not to mention my critically acclaimed performance as the Cowardly Lion in *The Wizard of Oz*. I was also nominated to run for class president, and though I didn't win, I loved saying, "It's an honor just to be nominated." Why does that line always sound so disingenuous?

Next up: surviving high school.

■

HIGH SCHOOL

nglewood Cliffs was so small that there weren't enough residents to warrant having our own high school. We had two grade schools and one middle school, but far be it from me to make any sense of decisions made by the Department of Education. For high school, I had two options. One was the nearby Dwight School for Boys, a private school that cost $5,000 per year, which in today's currency equates to $40,000. My parents loved me, but not $160,000 worth. We may have moved on up, but not to that stratosphere. My other option was getting bussed to Dwight Morrow, a public high school in the Fourth Ward of Englewood, one town over, that was predominantly African American. Some of my friends enrolled in the private school, and the rest of us boogied on down the hill to the real world.

On the first day of school, I sat quietly while the homeroom teacher took attendance. Out of nowhere, a black guy arriving late for class strutted into the classroom, took one look at my geeky self, poured a cup of hot tea on my lap, laughed, and then took his seat. Shocked and horrified and needing to not come off as a crybaby, I got up, walked to the teacher, said I needed to be excused, and walked out the door. It looked like I had peed my pants, adding to my fury. I hitchhiked a ride home, silently raged at my parents for cheaping out and putting me in this untenable situation. If that was day one, I wanted to avoid day two, day three, and certainly year four. I got dropped off a few blocks from my house and furiously stormed up the hill, still wet, getting angrier and angrier at the whole situation. My dad better cough up whatever money it took, because Dwight Morrow High School did not have my name on it.

I harrumphed up the brick stairs to the front door and banged on it with my fist. My mom answered, surprised to see me arriving back home within an hour of boarding the school bus.

"What are you doing here?" she asked.

"*YOU* can go to that high school. I'm out. Look."

I showed her my dungarees that, fortunately, were thick enough to have prevented a scalding on my thigh from the hot tea. But that was beside the point. "This schmuck poured boiling water on me. For no reason."

"Oh no! You poor baby." She gave me a big hug. "Go change your pants."

"Good idea," I said sarcastically and went up to my room, put on pajama bottoms, then headed downstairs to the TV room.

"Where do you think you're going?"

"Call Daddy and tell him I simply must go to Dwight School for Boys. I'm not going back to that place; I can tell you that."

"Oh yes, you are. Now get dressed and get in the car."

"Look at what happened to me on the first day."

"Dressed. Car."

Every fucking time anything happened that was emotionally challenging, I would automatically put it into perspective by thinking, "This should have been the worst thing that happened to her during the war." So you see? I could never escape the constant yielding to my mother's tragic past. It was a losing battle of wits, and always to my wit's end. Nothing I could ever do or say would have earned pity from my mother.

Begrudgingly, having lost the argument, I got into the car. We went down Palisade Avenue in the silver Chrysler 300, a Sherman tank of a car in which my petite mom was barely visible above the steering wheel as we arrived at the long, tree-lined entrance of the school grounds. Despite being a public school, Dwight Morrow shockingly resembled stately Princeton University. It was set on a 35-acre campus with manicured grounds featuring Miller's Pond, complete with ducks and fish, and Gothic architecture, including a massive bell tower reminiscent of the cathedrals in Milan.

I jumped out of the car, turned to my mother, gave her the evil eye, and walked up the long driveway. I didn't want anyone to see my "mommy" dropping me off. I was still deflated from that incident at homeroom; I could only imagine what fresh hell awaited me. My biology class was underway. Arriving late, it was shades of that fateful April Fools' grand entrance at the last school. I took a deep breath, swung the door open, this time with attitude, sniffed, "Sorry, I'm late. I overslept," and headed to the back of the room to take a seat. I sat beside Steve, whose sister Donna was one of my BFFs. Unlike me, he was a jock, whereas Donna and I enjoyed listening to music, smoking weed, and eating. Many nights after dinner, we'd walk up to the football field, that same one where Jessie and I had run away from the cops on that fateful day of the Moratorium to End the War in Vietnam. Donna and I would lay on the 50-yard line, smoke a couple of joints, and stare at the sky, wishing we were Carole King and James Taylor. We spoke of our hopes and dreams to create big lives, unlike the ones we were currently living.

Little by little, my classmates got wind of my sense of humor as I tossed out one-liners from the back of the room in English,

Spanish, Sociology, Science, and Modern European History classes. The problem with being bussed to a mixed-race school is that you are instantly recognized as "other" just by your skin color. Not to split hairs, but Jews, technically, are not white since we hail from the Middle East and Africa, depending on which aspect of our history you choose to follow. But trying to explain that to a high school kid who only sees black and white as you walk through the hallway is not an option. When I got dirty looks, what was I supposed to say? "Hey, man, I'm like you…only in the abstract." It's a non-starter.

Bullying was commonplace at Dwight Morrow. The school was so tough that we destroyed four different principals during my four years there. It was also the times we lived through because they were a-changin'. The social construct of the microcosm at the school reflected what was happening throughout the United States. Attending Dwight Morrow High School was akin to living in an urban jungle, and it wasn't enough to be a class clown because I still needed a way to protect myself. By Jove, I think I got it. I would start selling Quaaludes and hopefully become a welcome addition to Dwight Morrow's "High" and get a reputation for being cool.

SIDEBAR: For you poor dears who have never taken a Quaalude, it is hard to describe how amazing it felt. It was a sensual ride with no hangover. My friend Nancy said it best: "Quaaludes make you want to have sex with a tree." It had a chemical compound that induced your libido by releasing dopamine, or some equally delicious neurotransmitter, which must be why drugs are often referred to as "dope." Not as in stupid, but rather, like the hip-hop meaning of the word. Quaaludes enabled you to act out sexually with abandon.

The violence in my school reflected the civil unrest happening around the country in the early '70s. One by one, all the white kids who got bussed into this school were at risk of getting their asses whooped. One of my favorite films, *West Side Story,* aired on national television in late April 1971 when the Lehigh Valley, Pennsylvania, high school riot happened. Racial tension exploded and was all over the news. Sadly, the Sharks and Jets rumble reenactment happened the next day at Dwight Morrow.

It started as an argument that turned into a scuffle in our grand, 20-foot ceilinged cafeteria, complete with massive chandeliers from the 1930s when the building was constructed. The lovely setting was the backdrop for what devolved into an all-out war between the white and black kids. The fight began with two girls, and from there, it grew and kept growing, complete with jeering and name-calling and plenty of bitch-slapping. When the melee started, my friends and I moonwalked backward out the door to the parking lot and stayed out of harm's way. We had perfect seats for watching these morons whale on each other. At one point, twenty kids appeared out of nowhere, looking for trouble just to bust some heads.

My friends and I were smoking a joint; it was like watching a bad movie, and we were shocked at the angst and violence we witnessed. "Wow, man," was all we could muster. There was nothing else to say. Of course, the cops came, and we resumed our lives, but seeing that violence triggered something inside me. Sure, I'd seen violence in films, but this was different. Seeing the worst in people right there in front of me was as scary as listening to my mother's stories about human cruelty during World War II. I saw veins popping out in anger and watched as kids my age punched other kids. I'll never forget the sound of someone getting punched with a clenched fist. Later that day, we discussed the incident in Sociology class. It opened a dialogue that has stayed with me forever. The importance of empathy and dignity remains close to my heart, mainly because it was how I was raised. Dwight Morrow High School was the most significant teaching moment I have endured and carried forward.

Just about every white boy in Dwight Morrow got his ass whooped as a rite of passage, as it were. My special day took place on a sunny fall morning when I was running late, as usual, to Spanish class during my junior year. I stopped to take a quick drink from the water fountain built into the tiled wall. When my left foot was on the ground and my right leg in mid-air, a black guy bumped into my right leg in that split second. He immediately got huffy, shoved me, and got into my face. Startled, I looked behind him, and in the blink of an eye, three of his tall friends surrounded me. I knew that my time had come.

"Hey man, what the fuck you think you're doin', man?" the tall basketball-player-looking guy said.

"Just getting some water, bro," I nervously replied.

"You kicked me with your leg, man."

"No, I did not. I was just getting some water."

"Yes, you did."

"Okay, sorry. Hey, man, I gotta go to class."

These guys were at least a foot taller than me, and I was up against the water fountain. I could feel the rim of the sink in my back. I was scared and, more importantly, furious. I had worked way too hard cracking jokes, selling dope, and doing anything I could think of to be accepted through the years to be the recipient of this bullshit.

"I said I was sorry. I gotta go. I'm late, yo?" I think my voice cracked on the "yo."

I felt another shove, and before things got out of hand, I pushed my chest through the wall of tall, dark, handsome boys and said, "I said I was sorry, okay? God damn it! I'm sorry and I'm late."

I scurried down the hall, hopefully out of harm's way. I was scared shitless, yet still more pissed that this was happening. I refused to be like every other white boy who got his ass kicked. That ritual was going to stop with me. And besides, I am not white, remember? Not according to many leftists, Christian conservatives, and in this instance, me.

I could hear the squeaking sound of my sneakers on the polished wood floors, and I got angrier the farther I got from would-be attackers. Fortunately, I did not hear their footsteps following me, which was surprising and reassuring. That walk felt a mile long. I could hear the guys grumbling, and finally, with the echo of the high ceilings, I could make out what one of them said.

"Damn, that white boy's got balls."

And with that, I saved myself from the obligatory ass-whooping that every one of my friends had received. Dwight Morrow taught me an invaluable lesson in diversity and inclusion and prepared me for my continuing education in the School of Hard Knocks. If you look at my LinkedIn page, that's how my alma mater is proudly displayed. Dwight Morrow was a crash course in the real world and taught me how to act tough and walk tall, using offensive posturing as a defense mechanism. Never look people in the eye unnecessarily. I carry this philosophy to this day as I walk down city streets, because I under-stand that inviting unnecessary conflict and engagement is pointless. This lesson is especially important for gay people, in particular, when we are cruising the streets. We need to sharpen our skills at deter-mining who is available or who might be a potential assailant. The halls of my high school taught me critical lessons in self-preservation.

True grit was how I managed to win the conflict and resolution with those boys in the hallway, head held high. It became clear that life is a series of uphill battles, and your preparedness will determine the outcome. I needed to keep score of the wins and losses as a critically important, very personal dogfight loomed on my horizon: conquering the battle of the bulge. With all the marijuana and the food cravings that came with it, I was getting way too overweight for my own good. I looked like shit, and not even Quaaludes could soften the impact of what I saw in the mirror.

LOSING A HUMAN

Losing a human being can be an exhilarating experience. I'm not talking about losing an actual person such as a lover, friend, or family member, which tends to be a sad affair, though not always. Losing enough excess fat to equal the weight of an entire human being—now that's exhilarating. And that was yours truly. Such a loss—a person's worth of blubber—was something I was fortunate enough to experience. It was the gift I gave myself for my seventeenth birthday.

I attributed the amount of unwanted fat I'd gained throughout my childhood to having been stuffed to the gills by my overly Jewish mother. She must've figured that stuffing her son like a sausage would guarantee that if the Nazis had a resurgence in America, he could live off the fat of his loins rather than having to scrounge around the woods for a radish. Having a Holocaust-survivor mother lurking around every corner with a spoonful of chicken-fat-laden chopped liver is no one's idea of a carefree childhood.

Despite the damage caused by Holocaust nightmares and getting a good look at myself in the nude, one thing was clear: many pounds needed to go. Besides, I wanted to see my penis again. I was sick and tired of girdling into my dungarees. It was either lose weight or hara-kiri, and since I wasn't Japanese, that wasn't an option. Besides, you cannot do that to Holocaust survivor parents. The guilt would haunt you into the afterlife. This was a job for Superman or God.

> *Dear God,*
> *You must be sick and tired of people praying to you for stuff, especially when shit gets serious. But what I cannot fathom is that you let the Holocaust happen and linger on for years while millions of your loyal followers were pleading for you to put an end to the Nazi madness. If you do exist and heard their desperate cries for help, then chances are what I'm about to beg you for may also fall on deaf ears. Besides, if Genesis is true, and you made man in your image, which "man" do you look like? You can't possibly tell me that you're fat, short, and wear glasses. And if you do look like me, then how did a Robert Redford or a Paul Newman happen? And since male models exist, what the fuck did you do to me, and why? With that, I'm begging you to please help me look like a more desirable human being and free me from the bondage of my height, weight, and need for eyewear. And can you please, Lord, do something about my addiction to carbohydrates. I'm going to be a senior in high school; you must do something about this before yearbook pictures.*
> *Love,*
> *ABE*

And like a Christmas miracle or Moses' parting of the Red Sea, something extraordinary happened on March 15, 1973, the day that changed my life forever. Being the Quaalude-dealing class clown while resembling Mama Cass Elliot was not a tenable situation. It's worth noting that the Ides of March, the day Brutus killed Julius Caesar, was the official kick-off to my Battle of the Bulge.

That day, I met up with one of my steady customers, Michelle, an adorable, perfectly fit female specimen who was pontificating about the Dr. Atkins diet and announcing that she'd lost eight pounds in no time.

"But you already look amazing!" I admonished.

"I eat whatever and as much as I want on the 'Yes' list and none of what's on the 'No' list."

An awkward silence fell between us as a pink elephant lumbered around the room. Annoyed that Michelle had already looked great before her recent weight loss, I handed her a packet of Ludes; she winked, air-kissed me on both cheeks, and left me standing there feeling inadequate. How dare someone who was already in great shape go on a diet? How dare she even bring up the subject of dieting to me? How dare I *not* be dieting was the bigger question. I went home, stripped down nude, looked in the mirror, and, for the very first time, I sobbed at my appearance.

I was deeply ashamed of myself for letting things get to the point of self-disgust. I had known for years that being fat wasn't a good look. Although I was drowning in this pool of misery, keeping people laughing was the go-to coping mechanism that protected me from being judged on looks alone. I remember dreading the summers in the Catskills when everyone went swimming; I refused to go shirtless because all the other boys were thin. I would wear a white T-shirt and say it was to prevent sunburn, but that wasn't the case at all. I was convinced that it made me look, well, maybe not thinner, but less fat somehow. But the truth is that a wet T-shirt clinging to my body brought more attention to the flubber, not less. At moments like these, the denial mechanism kicks in at an early age and becomes the modus operandi of your ego-system. Over time, denial becomes a blindfold to your actions and, in my case, looks. Now the fragile blown-glass shell that had served as the barrier between me and the world had cracked, and the shards pierced my broken heart. My encounter with Michelle was like an earthquake erupting in my soul; it left me devastated, and the residual effects of what I was afraid to confront have never totally left me. Tiny little fragments of impending doom lurk around the corners of my mind.

I begged my sister to take me to the bookstore so I could buy a copy of *Dr. Atkins' Diet Revolution*. The diet involved cutting out all carbohydrates. Having just begged God to rid me of my obsession, the coincidence caught me by surprise. Had God heard me and not the Jews of Europe in the 1940s? Anyhoo, so began the transformation. The Dr. Atkins Diet became my obsession. At first, skepticism led me to challenge its viability. I decided to prove Michelle and Dr. Atkins wrong by overeating everything on the YES list.

Breakfast: 12 eggs, four slices of bacon

Lunch: 3 cans of tuna with mayo, and replace bread with American cheese slices

Dinner: Large steak and lamb chops. To my surprise, the diet actually worked. I had lost twelve pounds by the end of week two, and miraculously, Dr. Atkins had ripped the carbohydrates' chokehold tether from me. I knew that I could happily live without the French fries from the Cottage Inn truck stop on Route 9W. It would be just a matter of time before the only burden left for me to carry was not my stomach but the Holocaust guilt for my mother and the millions of European Jews whose prayers God had *not* answered. Once I shed the unsightly excess pounds, my image could fit within the frame of the full-length mirror hanging on the back of my bedroom door, and I'd happily see my penis again.

Besides, I was doubly incentivized to transmogrify my entire being. My sister, Vivian, was getting married in September, the same week that I'd be starting my senior year of high school, and I needed to make a grand entrance at both events. Why? Two reasons:

- All my bungalow colony friends, whom I hadn't seen since we moved on up several years earlier, would be there.
- Who wouldn't want to show up at school and not be recognized? I needed a mind-altering, transcendent "Who's that?" moment.

Six months later, with an amazing transformation under my belt (which was six notches smaller, to be exact), I entered Dwight Morrow sixty-five pounds lighter and five inches taller, with hair down to my shoulders and a visible, working penis.

September 8, 1973
Dear God,
Thanks.
Love,
ABE
P.S.…So help me; if you let a Holocaust happen now that I am finally getting laid, I will STOP BELIEVING IN YOU.

MY FATHER'S DEATH BED

The kitchen phone rang at 11:00 PM. I was hanging out in my basement, telling my friends Donna and Steve how horrible it had been to walk into my bedroom the night before last, where my father, for some ungodly reason, had chosen to lay down on my bed to take a nap. I told them that he rarely came into my room, yet there he was, gasping for air, clutching his chest, and pleading for help. My mother was finishing a Columbia University teaching program and doing homework in the kitchen, and I didn't want to alarm her. So I called 9-1-1 from the pink princess phone in my parents' room and ran back to my father with a cold compress. He was suffering a massive heart attack. I hadn't felt that helpless ever, and I still haven't to this day. Nothing had prepared me for that moment, especially if it would be his last.

The ambulance came within minutes, and I ushered the paramedics into my bedroom, having closed off the kitchen door, still shielding my mother from the tragedy happening in real-time. As they wheeled my father out the front door on that cumbersome stretcher, my mother heard the banging noise, appeared from the pocket door to the kitchen, and began screaming. I grabbed her hand and told her everything would be all right and that we needed to go to the hospital. That was how her Mother's Day came to an end.

Barreling through the quiet, rain-soaked streets like a madman, I couldn't shake the image of my father lying there, gasping for air. He was only fifty years old. Tears streamed down my face, blurring my vision. I had never developed a close relationship with him because he was always working, struggling to keep our family in the comfortable lifestyle he had provided for us. There was love between us, and our family was very affectionate, but few, if any, father-and-son bonding moments came to mind—nothing to hold onto.

After returning from a late Mother's Day lunch earlier that day, we'd had a terrible fight about something that I had discovered and had been keeping secret. Secrets are so toxic. They weigh on us, chaining us to the lies we must tell to protect those we love from the pain that the truth will undoubtedly cause.

Months before, I had discovered that my father was having an affair. I was keeping it secret because I didn't want to be the one to tell my mother. He had to tell her. The whole sordid situation felt shamefully and infuriatingly wrong. Not to mention how disrespectful it was to my mother. I didn't dare tell her, but I couldn't hold back the anger that had been building since I'd stumbled upon the fact that the man we revered so much had betrayed us so deeply. Watching him lie throughout the Mother's Day meal was becoming unbearable, and like a time bomb, I almost exploded at the restaurant but held back—to protect her. When we came home, I pulled him aside in the garage after my mother entered the house and blurted out that I knew everything and hated him for it. He naturally began denying everything I knew to be true, making the lies even worse. Staring him in the eyes, I told him when and how his dirty little secret had begun to unravel. I said terrible things in a tirade, not letting him speak.

The last words I had said to him before storming off were "I hope you drop dead." Dear God, what had I done? I didn't hope for that at all. Not now. Not then. Not ever. This couldn't possibly be his end.

I went through every red light until a police car came zooming up behind me, flashing its headlights to pull me over. Ignoring it, I passed yet another red light, leaving the cop no choice but to speed ahead and cut me off. As red flashing lights filled our car, my mother still sobbing uncontrollably, I shot out of the car before he could get out of his vehicle to swagger over and demand my license. I ran through the rain to the police car, tears rolling down my face.

"My father just had a heart attack, see that ambulance, he's in there; we gotta get to the hospital!"

The rugged-faced policeman immediately understood, turned on his siren, and said, "Get back in your car and follow me."

Chaos ensued over the next few hours which felt like days of suspended animation. We were waiting for something—anything— from the on-call doctor; asking the nurses for updates felt like we were a burden to the bored, overweight staff. We asked for Dr. Goldstein, who had cared for my father a few years prior when he'd had phlebitis. Even after midnight, he agreed to be jolted from his bed and attend to my dad. For some reason, this gave us hope. Within the hour, the big, round-faced, burly Dr. Goldstein pushed through the swinging doors, wearing a black overcoat and smoking a cigarette.

A few relatives had joined us in the dreary waiting room by then. After an endless while, Dr. Goldstein came out of the emergency room and told us that my father was not "out of the woods"—an expression that has never made sense to me. What about the woods is reminiscent of a catastrophic health scare? Woods were beautiful, and even if you got lost in them, give me the woods over the fear of coronary artery disease any day of the week. The doctor told us that my dad would be in intensive care for 72 hours, after which he would know more about his chances.

"Chances?" I didn't like the sound of that phrase.

A fog set in, and nothing would be clear for quite some time, as luck would have it—my luck. Bad luck, that is. We were told to go home and rest; we drank coffee as the sun rose and dragged around the house until we could return to the hospital during visiting hours. When I walked into my father's hospital room, he was still unconscious. I looked at him sleeping peacefully and prayed that he would open his eyes so I could say, "I'm sorry, please forgive me." We sat with him for hours, talked to him, hoping he could hear us tell him how much we loved him and wanted to see him smile. I wanted to look into those big, black, kind eyes, just like mine. I began to lose hope that he would survive. It was at that moment that I began to consider the afterlife. Perhaps I could resolve this insurmountable unresolved issue over what I had said to him. If not in the here and now, surely in the there and then.

At hour 36, my father had still not shown signs of knowing we were there. We were hoping and praying that by hour 72 he would be alert and out of the friggin' woods once and for all. My mother and I went home, sat silently at the kitchen table covered with her unfinished homework, and shared a pot of tea.

I thought back to the summer when I was eleven years old, after my father had discovered making money and had moved us "on up" from the dregs of Weehawken. I remember cornering him that summer and asking him to tell me about the facts of life. Since I was five, I had known all about the birds and bees, but I wanted to test his parenting skills. He told me, "We'll get a rowboat and go fishing on Swan Lake sometime this summer, and I'll tell you." He handed me a wad of twenties and left to play poker with his buddies. The summer came with no rowboat, fishing, or sex-planation. In hindsight, I would have been much happier just to have spent some alone time with him—a rarity, if ever—and to have skipped the sordid conversation.

My sister Vivian, my mother, and I decided not to call Rita, who was away at college finishing up her final exams. That's how confident we were that "this too shall pass" would take place. Only it didn't pass. My father did. I would never live down the guilt of not telling Rita, his favorite, to come home so she could be at his side, or in this case, at his deathbed.

So when the phone rang that night at 11 PM, 48 hours after this nightmare had begun, as I looked at my friends Donna and Steve, tears welled up. I knew it was bad news. The worst-case scenario was happening. The nurse suggested we come back to the hospital. Another hysterical ride to Englewood Hospital ensued; I ran ahead to the room where I had last seen my father and watched Dr. Goldstein working to massage my father's heart, pounding his chest, and finally, giving up. He was gone. Watching as he took his last breath, I stood over my father and cried. Dr. Goldstein handed me my father's wedding ring that he'd slipped off his finger and said he was sorry. He was not alone.

Sobbing, I went to the waiting room, where the news had just been shared with the rest of my family—a scene that's hard to relive to this day. Years earlier, my father had brought me a gift from Israel, a delicate blown glass charm that, translated to English, is the symbol that means life. I loved it and wore it close to my heart. When my father died, I ripped the chain off my neck and stomped on the blown glass charm that meant life. I looked out the window, up toward the sky, and swore off God with all his bullshit.

That night, I tossed, turned, and finally fell into a deep sleep after taking my third sleeping pill. I floated off into dreamland where a big green dragonfly led my father and me down a narrow, wooded path to the edge of a calm, unspoiled lake. The dragonfly was buzzing and ricocheting as it flew ahead of us. We arrived at a once-burgundy, now-weathered rowboat anchored along the rocks, and together, we lifted the nose of the boat. I hopped in as he eased it gently into the water and then he joined me on the boat, creating delicate, rippling waves that shattered the shimmering reflection of the scorching summer sky. We rowed slowly toward the center of the lake as a majestic eagle soared overhead with stunning, overpowering grace, calling, screeching, demanding to know who dared enter her lair. Finally, we arrived where I had always wanted to be. Alone. With him. No sisters, no mother, no histrionics, no customers, no poker buddies, no one. Just my father and me. I had spent eleven years waiting for my turn. We cast our rods and, in doing so, cast a shadow on the lives of the unsuspecting innocent creatures swimming below.

In silence, we took in the splendor of the day and the grandeur of the dinosaur-shaped, purple mountains in the distance. The sun beat down, bronzing our arms and reddening our noses, while a clean, crisp, fresh, intoxicating aroma rose from the water. I cupped my fingertips along the lake's surface, dabbed the back of my neck as I felt it reddening from the sun, and was stopped by my father's disapproving eye. "Don't; you'll scare away the fish," he said in his thick, European accent, the first words he had uttered that morning. There was so much to talk about, and yet nothing much to say. I could never make idle chit-chat with my father, unlike the ease I felt while prattling on and on with my mother and sisters about everything and nothing.

My father was my gentle giant—hard-working, generous, and kind. He was my hero who made Herculean choices during World War II that are inconceivable to me. As a teenager in Warsaw, he was imprisoned in a Siberian gulag, escaped, found his way back to Germany, and, in yet another unfathomable life choice, joined the Underground. That was about all I knew. Unlike my mother, he wasn't one to talk about his life or war experiences, and I wondered if those days were distant memories now. Perhaps they still haunted him: unspeakable, horrific memories, thoughts, and visions floating on the water's surface.

I've been told that you should never meet your heroes, as they will always disappoint. Who are your heroes now that politicians have proven untrustworthy, celebrities are not different from us, and caped crusaders are only heroes for pay? What would we say to our heroes anyway? When I realized that my father was the only true hero I would ever encounter in my life, what would I say to him if given a chance to have one brief conversation before he slipped away?

- Thank you.
- Was magnificence a choice?
- Please give me your strength.
- Help me to be more like you.
- Tell me what happened.

The flapping tail of a large striped perch startled me. My father reeled in the doomed, flailing fish with ease and dexterity, unhooking it and passing it to me. I froze, swallowed, and flung the dying fish in the cooler. We smiled, he winked, and I laughed. The rest of the afternoon was spent in the peaceful embrace of the delicious silence, all the while knowing that we were total opposites yet somehow so very much alike. The sun was almost gone now. It was time to call it a day, dock the boat, say goodbye to the calm, unspoiled lake and what would have been the best thing on Earth to have done at least once before he died. I hated waking up from this place of peace and tranquility to the harsh reality that we had to plan his funeral.

Rest in peace

A GUCCI CLINCHER

t wasn't until I went to Italy that fatefully delicious summer that it became clear, and there was no denying it anymore, that I preferred sleeping with men. I was nineteen years old and had planned to travel to the south of France for a week with my sister, her friend Susan, and my straight friend Rob. We'd discussed our plans during the winter, but when it came time to book reservations in April for a July trip, Rita and Rob flaked out. Though we had only met once briefly, Susan and I decided to move forward with the trip anyway. We arrived at JFK with very little to say to each other, but fortunately, I had brought several icebreakers (a.k.a. Quaaludes). I was determined to have a grand old time. We were on a chartered flight with 88-year-olds, and I noticed another young couple waiting in the lounge. We introduced ourselves.

David and Elise were on their honeymoon, staying in Cannes, whereas Susan and I were headed to the Hotel Negresco in Nice. The flight was delayed, so we ordered a round of drinks. I hinted at having brought some drugs; they, too, had a stash. (Come on; it was the '70s!) We switched seats with a couple of codgers to be near each other during the long flight, and by the time we all got off on our first Quaaludes, we were professing our love for one another, hugging and kissing.

We landed at the Côte d'Azur, slightly disheveled, hugged and kissed our new friends goodbye, and went our separate ways.

"You think that marriage will last?" I asked Susan.

We checked into the hotel and then went for a walk on the Promenade des Anglais, catching up with ourselves and making plans. We dined at the world-class Le Chantecler restaurant on foie gras and bouillabaisse, and, for the first time, I felt as though I had transcended into the madding crowd to arrive where Mick, Bianca, and Marianne spent countless hours sucking on lobsters' claws and then some.

The next day, after strolling around the Old Town for hours and having another sumptuous meal and downing two bottles of rosé, we returned to the Negresco, made love, and took a nap. We decided to call our friendly honeymooners staying at the Hotel Carlton and taxied to see them. We drank, ate dinner, did Ludes, and enjoyed each other for dessert. It all seemed so natural, this living in the fast lane, enjoying sexual freedom with complete abandon. After a day of non-stop quadra-marital bliss, the four of us rented a car and drove to Florence, Italy, like we were living in a François Truffaut film.

Knowing I would be near the Gucci flagship store, my mother had begged me to bring her back a "pocketbook," which is what "It Bags" used to be called in the '70s. Driving through the countryside of France and Italy was so overwhelmingly beautiful that we stopped along the way and enjoyed each other's company, a new kind of picnic if you know what I mean. We pulled into Florence and were overwhelmed with the beauty and splendor of the city. We walked across the Ponte Vecchio, saw the statue of David, visited countless piazzas and grand churches, and sobbed from the city's splendor. We entered the impressive flagship Gucci store, where personal shopping guides approached the four of us.

Guests were personally escorted through the store with a chaperone, the height of customer service. It seemed that the store's policy was that each client would have a personal shopper with them of the opposite sex. Since childhood, being relegated to the husky department and not wanting to talk about my waist size, I have been a self-contained shopper and still hate it when salespeople follow me around, trying to be nice. My lovely, blonde female sales associate was not taking the hint that I wanted to peruse the store alone. Finally, she turned to me and said, "Oh, I get it. Wait here." In a flash, a tall, stunning male creature clad head-to-toe in Gucci appeared. He had crystal-blue eyes, black tousled hair, and an Australian accent. My heart sank deep into my groin.

"Hello, I'm Roberto."

Roberto wore a fitted black suit and a chartreuse silk shirt unbuttoned enough to show his manly chest hair. Intoxicated by his subtle masculine fragrance, I became weak in the knees. Suddenly, angels were singing. The blonde winked, and Roberto and I took a long, romantic stroll through Gucci-land. My heart began to flutter. We started at the pocketbooks, perusing the wares as my mother's order rang in my head. As I gazed into the limpid pools of Roberto's blue eyes, he showed me handbag after handbag. With each one, I kept saying, "I'll take it," never looking away from his face. After realizing I had said yes to five different pocketbooks, I knew I'd have to figure out a tasteful way to put a couple back. Just not yet. I would buy one for my mother, and if it meant I could stare at Roberto a bit longer, I was willing to buy two more, one for each sister. But that was my limit. I wanted to extend this dance as long as I could. During the '70s, Italian men carried little purselets with a hand strap under their armpits. Roberto pulled one out for me to consider, but I responded, "It's not my thing. Not that there's anything wrong with guys who wear purses, mind you. It's just not my look." He winked at me; I swooned.

Let's discuss my look for a moment. I had long, curly hair that fell below my shoulders. I wore a tight black T-shirt, Levi's 501 Button-Fly jeans, and a pair of navy suede clogs. Somehow, I didn't realize I looked like a Greenwich Village queen, even though everyone who looked at me, like the blonde female chaperone who first joined me in the Gucci store, knew at first glance. I didn't yet know about gaydar. Roberto, my knight in Gucci shining armor, must've sensed it immediately, too. I wanted him to chaperone me for eternity and was happy to find out there were three floors that would extend my time with him. Suddenly, shopping alone seemed so sad.

Without hesitation, I added two belts to the pile and agreed to try on a pair of those famous Gucci loafers similar to the ones he was wearing. Prince Charming caressed my foot and gently slipped it into the shiny, black loafer with the iconic gold, double G logo. "Sold."

We checked out blazers, which didn't go with my look, then sauntered toward the swimwear department. He started going through the rack, turned to me, and said, "Do you like chartreuse?" Anything in chartreuse, I thought to myself as he grabbed a teeny-tiny chartreuse number. We went up to the dressing rooms on the third floor, where all the sales associates brought their clients. No one else was up there at that moment, so before I could slip into the bathing suit after completely disrobing, Roberto entered the dressing room and stared into my eyes. He planted his thick lips on mine. We proceeded to make out passionately as my better angel left my body and hovered, recording this liaison for posterity and proof. And it was at that moment, while stone-cold sober (a rarity for me) with this stunning creature, I finally knew that this was how I wanted to feel for the rest of my life, preferably twenty-four hours a day.

I heard the others calling for me, and I had to end our brief but life-affirming close encounter of the hottest kind. We said our goodbyes (mine teary), and I returned to my friends. In all the excitement, I had forgotten that I had agreed to purchase a carload of Gucci accouterment. I met Roberto at the concierge desk to pay for the merch that I definitely did not need. I ended up buying three bags, two belts, shoes, and a scarf, passing on the chartreuse bikini bottom. The others sensed the connection between Roberto and me, and they inched closer, trying to hear our last words together. Roberto quietly asked if I was staying in Florence overnight and if we could get together. With regret, I said no (but talk about gift-with-purchase).

Having had the most miraculous summer vacation of my life, it was clear that I needed to let the cat out of the bag and finally tell my family. The timing was genius; I could hand out these pocketbooks as goodie bags to soften the blow. I mean…what better coming-out party favor is there than a Gucci goody bag?

YOU KNOW YOU'RE GAY WHEN…

You know what color chartreuse is.
You have used chartreuse in a sentence.
You wear chartreuse.

For millions of red-blooded American boys and girls—heck, not just Americans but anyone in the world with red blood—coming out of the closet to your family takes a bit of doing. Perhaps "takes a bit of doing" is putting it mildly, since one tends to agonize over the decision to the nth degree…or it is to the nth power? Regardless, it hurts. But it hurts so much that you start thinking that if you don't say something out loud, if you don't make the declaration audible enough for your whole family to hear you, and have them understand what it is you are trying to say—between beating around the bush and stuttering your way through a critical, soon-to-be-spewed (think Linda Blair in *The Exorcist*) proclamation of gayness, if you don't get it out before you explode, you will have every right to lay the blame at their feet. There. You did it. You just sort of blamed your family for being "a gay" (as my mother would say). Everything else is their fault, so why not add your homosexuality to the list? Just throw it on the pile.

Sit-down family meetings conjure up many different outcomes. If your maiden voyage for such an undertaking is to utter the words,

"I am a homosexual," there are two ways this conversation can go. Since even writing those words is hugely uncomfortable, imagine what it must feel like to utter them, since they don't fall trippingly off the tongue. We tend to put off saying them for as long as possible, especially to ourselves. Asking the family to gather together already seems awkward, like the last time it happened, which was never. Such moments rarely end with great news. Our family meetings never ended with, "We won Ed McMahon's Lottery." Riveting topics like which hotel in the Catskills we would stay at for the Jewish Holidays or what flavor of ice cream my father should bring home were the big concerns at my family's version of the Knights of the Round Table.

There was that one time when I requested a family sit-down meeting to announce that I had totaled my father's brand-new Oldsmobile. I had taken it without his permission on the one and only day I can remember that he had stayed home because he was too sick to go to work. To add insult to injury (thankfully there weren't any injuries but plenty of insults), I was cutting class with several friends with the genius plan of copping drugs and hanging out in Washington Square Park for the afternoon. The day was a total loss since I cracked up the car before even getting on the damn George Washington Bridge. The reason I wanted my whole family to attend that sit-down was to secure a pity vote from my mother. I was guaranteed a melodramatic, shrill sigh of relief that I was not dead and no one else was hurt other than the car itself. Her shrill response might protect me from my father's wrath. My father, on the other hand, was far more upset about the car being destroyed because he knew that with my mother in the room, he could not do what he really wanted to do, which was to smack me hard across the face. He must have resented me for being under the constant protection of my mother. She would never let him lay a hand on me.

At the risk of sounding gruesome, it was lucky for me that my dad had died before I called for this awkward family meeting. Yes, lucky, because I couldn't imagine the über awkwardness of telling my über masculine father that I was gay and all that implies. Let's just say that I wished more than anything for my father to be alive, just not on that particular day.

It took years for me to cobble together enough gumption to come out of the closet to my family. I reflected back to when I began to wonder quietly, "Oy vey, am I a homosexual or what?" It started around the time I first watched *The Wizard of Oz*, which shook me to the core for many reasons. Why did those three farmhands live together on Dorothy's farm? Wasn't Professor Marvel a tad too flamboyant, with similar inflections to mine? Let's not discuss how nelly the Cowardly Lion was, while we're on the subject. Was Glenda the Good Witch talking directly to me in secret code when she sang, "Come out, come out, wherever you are"? And don't get me started on how the gay community's obsession with Judy Garland led to co-opting the "over the rainbow" rainbow.

My 8th grade theatrical debut as the Cowardly Lion. Coincidence, I don't think so.

> SIDEBAR: For years, I questioned the hideous rainbow flag as it clashed with everything I wore, even with all black. Might I suggest we replace it with a tasteful, fifty shades of gray, dip-dyed number. But I digress.

If you ask me, Almira Gulch was a lesbian and had been in love with Auntie Em since grade school. Who knows what could have happened one drunk night? When Almira shows up to take Toto away, it shows how vindictive she is, like a jilted lover. What was she hoping to hear: "Leave Toto, take me instead?" There's a lot of unresolved sexual tension in that scene, with Uncle Henry awkwardly bumbling around, not knowing what to say or do or where to look. He probably knew about their past. Why else would Auntie Em say, "For twenty-three years, I've been dying to tell you what I thought of you! And now, well, being a Christian woman, I can't say it!" Notice how she didn't say "good Christian woman." *The Wizard of Oz* is all about punishment and torment, which is what happens to just about every character in the movie. Excuse me for thinking that going home is not necessarily a happy ending.

Having *The Wizard of Oz* stuck in my craw and being oddly attracted to Jack La Lanne in kindergarten were sure signs that things might not go swimmingly during my teenage years. That seminal moment sizing up Jack's gray, high-waisted, albeit-belted jumpsuit had me wondering, "Shit, am I going to have to troll through gymnasiums my whole life to get my ya-yas out?" Homosexual thoughts, looking like a Munchkin, and having secret crushes on Lyle Waggoner and the Bionic Man made me feel like an outcast. Besides, I was plenty jealous of Farrah Fawcett. Not only did she marry Lee Majors, but she was tall, blonde, rich, and thin—virtually everything I aspired to become.

Could I will her into obscurity? Lord knows she did get booted from *Charlie's Angels* after one season, though every straight boy had her iconic poster in that red bathing suit on his bedroom ceiling for years to come.

While doing some digging into my family history, I learned about an "artist" cousin on my mother's side of the family, born in Russia, who had moved to Paris before World War II, leaving behind his wife and child in Poland to pursue his dreams. His name was Leonardo, though I bet he was born Sergei. The whole thing sounded sordid and can be misconstrued as a kind of gay move. Either way, Leonardo put himself and his family in an awkward position: between a rock and a hard-on.

The time had come. My sister Rita was still living at home when I summoned her and my mother to the kitchen table for our "chat." I called Vivian and asked her to join us, and while we waited for her, I cut up a chocolate marble cake from Michelle's Bakery and poured cups of Sanka. Vivian arrived shortly thereafter, and we ate and drank while I beat around the bush until I finally blurted out, "Look, I gotta tell you guys something."

My mom, who must've remembered the last time I called for one of these sit-down sessions, said, "Not another car accident, Abie, for God's sake."

"No, Ma, not that. Well…(dramatic pause)…remember Sharon's friend David, the opera singer?"

Vivian had met him once. "Barely."

"Didn't I tell you he asked me to be an extra in Puccini's *Turandot* at Lincoln Center?"

That piqued my mother's interest. "Opera?"

Rita looked at me blankly. "What do you mean? What's a Turandot?"

They all looked at me like I was nuts. Perhaps I had never told them about that one crazy night that evolved from a brief affair with Sharon's friend. David was the second lead in the City Opera production, and he told the director to add me to the cast as one of the supernumeraries, which are the extras on stage in full regalia. No singing would be required for me as one of the extras in *Turandot*.

Before my great Lincoln Center debut, I was feeling very flu-ish by midday. I called David to say I wasn't feeling well, but he insisted I buck up: "This is the theater, the show must go on." By curtain, I and several other priests wearing full drag with a massive headdress had only one task: to walk slowly on and off stage in a procession. At that point I must have had a 103-degree fever, and as we slowly walked in single file from stage left to right, I swayed off the line while trying desperately to keep the headdress in place. It had to have been notice-able from the audience that I was doing Carmen Miranda meets I Love Lucy while trying to balance this monstrosity of a headdress. That was the beginning and end of my theatrical career.

"New York City Opera?" Vivian questioned.-

"What…?" My mother, who we have established was a coloratura soprano in her youth, showed a bit of excitement at the mere mention of the word *opera*.

"Never mind that…I'm gay."

"No kidding," Rita and Vivian both replied in stereo.

My mother immediately interjected, "I love Puccini."

Did she hear what I had just said? I wondered. Was she in denial, too?

"Ah…it's a phase."

This is what I'd been torturing myself over? Worrying for nothing. For coming out to your family, gay people deserve a special kind of medal for bravery. Move over, Purple Heart—make room for the

Pink Heart in recognition of years of holding it in. Kinda like how it felt like that time you couldn't get the key in the lock fast enough and nearly peed your pants. The rest of our coffee klatch continued with our usual, hilarious banter, and I was relieved of the secret I'd kept for years.

WHEN PIGS FLY

ave you ever wondered how different life might be if specific incidents hadn't happened? Is life ruled by fate, free will, or is it all just a bad reality show? Since there are no do-overs, what becomes your truth is how you respond to certain events that become life-changing and, sadly, not necessarily in a good way. I went from being a carefree party boy enjoying my senior year of high school to a traumatized, absolutely unforgivable charlatan.

Trying to make sense of my father's untimely, unexpected death was something I would never fully come to terms with. At least, not for the foreseeable future. That first Sunday morning after we buried my dad, I took it upon myself to take his car and get bagels to bring home to the family, as was his ritual. The gesture was something I hoped would bring them—and me—some comfort. When I returned and spread out the bagels and the three kinds of cream cheese we liked, my intention was to bring home a piece of our father to share. Evoke a memory. The reaction was lukewarm at best. We ate in silence, and as much as I had hoped to be like my dad, it was clear that I would never come remotely close. I'd be damned if I did and damned if I didn't.

Stuck in no-win limbo with a new, crippling, even-lower self-esteem issue. Need I remind you of the tireless desperation to confront and tackle my insecurities from being overweight my whole life? I had enjoyed barely one year of being the new me. My dad's death was a nail in my emotional coffin. No matter what I would accomplish in my life, it would never hold a candle to what he had done in his. Not even close. Especially since my only accomplishment to date had been losing sixty-five pounds and getting into Studio 54.

I was haunted by the terrible things I had said to my father, unable to get my own voice out of my head, coupled with the moving image of my dad lying in my bed, suffering. Just what I needed: more Jewish guilt. The guilt that comes with Jewish motherhood was more than enough to deal with. But this new layer of Jewish fatherhood guilt was catastrophically bound to put a crimp in my style and have a chilling, lingering effect on my psyche. This deep torment would need much more than Seconals or Quaaludes to numb the pain.

We devoured the bagels and retreated to our separate rooms to sulk. Thank God, though not technically anymore, I was going away to college in the fall and could hopefully escape my demons there. I hadn't realized yet that there was no escaping them. Jewish suburban boys are born with the expectation of becoming a doctor or a lawyer. One thing was certain: my father did not want me to follow in his footsteps by running an auto parts business in Secaucus, New Jersey.

One of the few memories of quality time I shared with my dad took place shortly after my bar mitzvah. He had taken me to his new warehouse, where he spent most of his waking hours. Now that I was technically a man, at least in biblical terms, it was time for the father-son outing I'd always yearned for. We drove down the New Jersey Turnpike in an awkward silence that had become the norm. More than anything, I wanted to feel at ease with him and talk about sports or politics, but for whatever reason, I, the loudmouth of the century, could not scramble together enough words to put us both at ease. I fiddled with the radio, trying to find a song to break the silence. As I turned the dial, I heard "Take It Easy" by The Eagles, a song I knew he liked. We shared a brief moment and sang the chorus, but the song ended too soon.

The smell of the New Jersey swampland permeated my father's brand new, gold Delta 88 Oldsmobile. The new-car smell couldn't disguise the world-renowned stench of the turnpike. Once we exited the highway to get to my dad's warehouse, we had to drive through the Meadowlands, which sounded prettier than they were because they were swamps. Endless acres of tall, willowy, grass-like flora that looked like tumbleweeds growing from the wet ground.

We arrived at Penhorn Avenue, which wasn't an avenue at all. Before we turned down the unpaved road, the iconic Secaucus landmark, Krajewski's Bar, sat at the corner. Above the historic watering hole was a rusty old train trestle with a peeling billboard from a time gone by that said, "Henry Krajewski for President, 1952, The Poor Man's Party." At that time, Henry Krajewski was the President of the Pig Farmers Association, and one could imagine he was the King of the Swamps. Henry Krajewski became a household name in New Jersey when he ran again in 1956 against Adlai Stevenson and Dwight D. Eisenhower. Henry changed his party affiliation to the America Third Party and took an even bigger beating despite offering free beer to his potential voters. He subsequently ran for governor as well, and lost, making him a three-strikes-you're-out loser. In reporting Krajewski's death, the *Sunday Times of Trenton* wrote that the perennial candidate "proved that anyone can run for president." How true and sad those words are, especially when we see who won years later—Donald Trump, the Gross

Baboon who is intent on abandoning democracy and bringing America to her knees. But I digress. :)

My father's business was situated in the center of what had once been Krajewski's hog heaven. At the end of the long road that went on for what seemed like a mile, we bounced up and down through potholes and arrived at a gray cinder-block building that could have passed for a prison if it wasn't for a giant yellow sign with black letters proclaiming Sivar Industries. Jews have this habit of naming their businesses with a combination of letters using family names. Miramax Films combines Miriam and Max, the parents of the criminal Harvey Weinstein. My mother was the one who came up with the acronym and willingly left her name out of it. Simon, Vivian, Abe, and Rita were Sivar.

The company was buzzing with a dozen or so young, male, blue-collar workers. Unbuttoned plaid shirts on top of wife-beaters, tight Wrangler jeans, Yankee caps, the unofficial uniform of Sivar Industries. The guys, I noticed, were all quite handsome, and this was another inkling that I was strangely attracted to men. It was incredibly awkward being the boss's son. The guys were extra friendly, but I'm sure they resented this short, chubby character to whom they needed to be cordial.

My dad had developed an exceptional rapport with his crew. They joked around and had much to discuss with him because business came first with my dad. The men came into his office one by one with issue after issue. They were like the butch sons he didn't have. Though it would be years before I came out, surely one of these guys must have noticed me trying not to stare at them. As of that day, I knew deep down that something was off, but I kept stuffing down my feelings with food as it was a lot to digest—the gay thing, not the food. I sat in my father's oversized, leather swivel chair in the smoke-filled, wood-paneled office and hoped all of this would never be mine one day.

We walked out to the cavernous warehouse filled with brown cartons and pallets of rolled steel. The metal was cut down to pieces and assembled into muffler clamps and tailpipe hangers. Each week, pallets of finished goods were shipped to the Chrysler Company in Detroit. My father had a contract with his second cousin, whom I had met at my bar mitzvah. I had been envious of his height, wishing I had inherited that gene. I walked up and down the maze of cartons stacked ten feet high and was given a ride on the forklift by my dad's right-hand man, Jeff. He smelled like freshly smoked cigarettes and coffee. I wanted to ride on that forklift for the rest of my life.

Years later, after I inherited my dad's business, Jeff and I worked late and shared a few beers. He told me a story about one of those deliveries to Detroit when he had pulled into a truck stop to "catch some shuteye." He said a guy had knocked on the door of his truck. It was as though he was admitting to having a sexual liaison with another man without telling me all the details. It felt like he was coming out or on to me. Something. My gaydar went off, but I had enough sense to know not to mix business with pleasure.

My father had a surprise for me when I returned to the office after my joy ride around the warehouse. At that time in suburbia, all the pre-pubescent boys were riding Honda motor scooters, which was my introduction to status symbols. When you lived among the little princes, you needed to show something off. The problem was that the gift my dad gave me wasn't a Honda. It was an off-brand, weird-looking electric bike that would never do. He sensed my disappointment, and what could have been a sweet gesture turned into yet another awkward moment. He threw the bike in the trunk, and we rode home along the stinky turnpike in a deafening silence that, to this day, makes me sad.

STUDIO 54

t was "the only" time and the best couple of years of my life. Studio 54 opened its doors to much fanfare in April 1977. My sister Rita read about the opening night party on Page Six of the *New York Post* in an article splashed with paparazzi shots of Bianca Jagger, Liza Minelli, and assorted glitterati. Rita was determined to get through those velvet ropes and muscle her way into the club alongside the in-crowd. The article mentioned that the two owners, Steve Rubell and Ian Schrager, were Jewish and single, which meant she was hell-bent on getting into the club against all odds. The second night after it opened, we schlepped into the city decked out in head-to-toe black and tried to make our way through the throng of oglers and onlookers.

The infamous doorman, Marc, was standing on a drainpipe under the black deco marquee, swathed head-to-toe in Aryan arrogance, emotionless, avoiding eye contact with anyone. He hovered over the swarm of bees—the wanna-bees, that is—heat-seeking for the lucky few that would be granted entrée through the pearly gates of what everyone who was anyone was calling the latest heaven here on earth. Getting into Studio was everything.

People were desperately calling "Marc!" from every direction. The crowd reminded me of the angry mob of crazed villagers in the movie *Young Frankenstein,* sans torches. They were raging with fury about being denied entry into the kingdom. Rita bulldozed through the horde of hopeful wannabes and maneuvered us closer to the front of the pack. "Marc!" she called over hundreds of other shouters and was immediately noticed because she was such a looker. Marc motioned for her to breeze through the velvet ropes. She grabbed my arm and we were whisked past the chaotic throng of disco devotees into a dark corridor. I remember looking back at the crestfallen people outside and thinking, "What a bunch of losers."

Was it looks or luck that got us in? Not everyone was allowed entry with their plus one. Steve Rubell, the club's Quaalude-addicted master-of-ceremonies, was notorious for—among many other things— splitting couples up, letting one in and not the other, leading to many ruined friendships and divorces. Lovers and friendships be damned. Perhaps these fundamentals of human relationships might make for a new category on *Jeopardy:* Things You Can Definitely Live Without.

We sashayed in with the beautiful people, and life would never be the same. I had stepped through The Looking Glass. The centerpiece of the elaborate, beveled-mirrored foyer was an enormous Art Deco crystal chandelier. There was a buzz in the crowd of hushed voices. Everyone looked at everyone, wondering who was who among the Who's Who— and an unrecognizable, electrifying feeling surged through my body. Everyone was beautiful, and suddenly, I felt beautiful. And validated. When we walked those few yards from the dirty street to this dark, sensual world, something changed. Until then, I was nobody. But not anymore. Now I was somebody. Who? I didn't know yet—but some-body, nevertheless. Little did I know it was the beginning of a lifelong journey to answer that question. For that brief moment, at least, I felt like I was someone special.

PHOTO: *Miestorm*

Situated in the soundstage of what was The Ed Sullivan Theater, the vast Studio 54 club was like nothing I'd ever seen. The bar was black, silver, and mirrored. The carpet was black; the couches were black-and-silver leather. Sarcophagus-sized vases containing elaborate floral arrangements were everywhere. The bartenders were stunning, and the dance floor was enormous and packed with celebrities, including Liza and Bianca, Halston, Andy Warhol, Lauren Hutton, and Calvin Klein; it was an endless parade of the fabulii. I knew Rita was in seventh heaven. I was still cooing about the fact that I was officially someone. In my own mind, anyway. The evening was magical—the atmosphere…intoxicating, as was the alcohol. And the Quaaludes didn't hurt. We danced, met tons of people, and didn't want to leave. People were making out all over the place. It was so decadent. The women's bathroom was the coolest place to hang out. I was hobnobbing with the madding crowd.

Suddenly, I noticed a beautiful woman with an unmistakable face I couldn't place. "Oh, my God!" Could that be Jessie from middle school? It would have been hard not to notice her, because she was a ravishing blonde with the latest Coupe Sauvage haircut by Didier. She had the same unforgettable piercing, luminous green eyes. Wearing a black patent leather trench coat, collar up, she was holding onto the wall for dear life.

"Jessie?"

No response.

"It's me, Abe. Jessie?"

She looked at me cross-eyed because she was shit-faced. Swaying, she gazed at me, trying to focus, and almost toppled over in her 5-inch Charles Jourdan stilettos. And just like that first time we had met years earlier on the football field of the middle school, I grabbed her before she could fall and was transported back to that life-affirming day. People were snorting and passing around a plate of cocaine, and I made sure Jessie got a few bumps. After she came to, we began to catch up. Since I didn't look the same as I had in seventh grade, it took a moment for her to recall our chance meeting years earlier. Rita, who was being chatted up by several handsome gentlemen, joined us, and the three of us returned to the dance floor to revel as the now-iconic cocaine-snorting, crescent moon art installation emerged every so often, to the crowd's delight. Brooke Shields, Michael Jackson, Cher, Farrah Fawcett… if you weren't at Studio, you didn't matter. We didn't want the night to end, but alas, guess where I had to be at 8 AM? Secaucus, New Jersey, was calling my name—reality bites.

Jessie lived in the same building as Marc, so we had no problems getting in after that night. Shortly after, Rita met a successful real estate developer and got off the disco merry-go-round. As for Jessie and I, we became thick as thieves, Studio 54 Club Kids, party buddies, and not much else, which was fine, since technically I was gay. At least we danced away many nights at Studio, which was leagues beyond those dismal basement house parties in the 'burbs of New Jersey.

Sadly, whenever I left our festive nights at Studio, I got a pit in my stomach because of the buzz-killing reality of being a not-so-lucky sperm club member relegated to the swampy pig farms to work. Where was the justice? I was a prisoner, chained to someone else's idea of who I should be while careening out of control in all aspects of my life: professionally, emotionally, sexually, and pharmaceutically. Something had to give.

JOANIE TOOK A SHIT

hy couldn't my father have left me a trust fund? Would that have been too much to hope for? Especially since we had moved on up. Instead, I got stuck with an albatross, a *farkakte* auto parts factory manufacturing muffler clamps and tailpipe hangers in the swamplands of New Jersey.

My sisters guilted me into dropping out of college after my freshman year at Boston University, where I was having the time of my life. We were trying to salvage the family's quasi-fortune-ish to maintain my mother's lifestyle. It was unfortunate and unfair because every Jewish suburban brat got to go through at least four years of partying… I mean, higher education. Many of my Englewood Cliffs classmates earned master's degrees and quite a few doctorates as well. I would be a college dropout; there is no way my dad would have wanted that for me.

Dear God,

Now do you see why I don't believe in you anymore? As if killing off my dad wasn't bad enough? Now this? How is this my new life as opposed to being a full-time Club Kid at Studio 54? Thanks for nothing. Stephen Hawking was right when he said, "There is no God."

Toodles,

ABE

I tried taking classes at Fairleigh Dickinson University in Teaneck, New Jersey. That was a fairly ridiculous effort in futility since I already had two full-time careers: running the family dynasty and being a Studio 54 Club Kid. Liberal Arts classes seemed pointless. Besides, Studio 54 was the best Sociology, Psychology, and Sex Ed class ever. My stint at Sivar Industries was a crash course in Business Management that would rival any university since no school offered that level of intense on-the-job training. I had to learn the ins and outs of the business in one summer, and for two years, working in earnest, I managed to keep the company afloat—in fact, thriving. However, it was at the expense of my sanity. Coming out as gay at the same time I was managing a very strait-laced auto parts company was taking its toll. I had tasted the jet-set nightlife that I had pined for as a kid and desperately wanted to live the unconventional lifestyle that the people I met at Studio 54 were living. It was the convergence of three non-congruent realities, which was too much to bear. My mental health was at stake, or my life; one or the other had to go.

And then, as it did for so many drug-addled disco bunnies, the crash happened. It's hard to make this long, convoluted story short, mainly because it involves a life crisis that convinced me to believe there was nothing to live for and no way out of my predicament. I'm not being a drama queen, either. My life seemed hopelessly pointless, in a theater of the absurd kind of way, thanks to a series of bad choices that painted me into a corner at a warehouse in Secaucus, New Jersey.

I'd been burning the candle at both ends since Studio 54 opened, and the buzz had begun to wear off. I was crumbling under the pressure of my dual existence as my straight-by-day act collided with my gay-by-night shenanigans. Let's not forget the tremendous responsibility I had at work to do more than just keep the lights on—namely, to maintain my mother's lifestyle. While I continued to act like I didn't have a care in the world, things were beginning to unravel. Need I reiterate the copious amount of drugs I was consuming to keep up with both demanding schedules?

Something snapped in my brain. Distraught, I went to Rita to tell her I was having a nervous breakdown. She had the good sense to immediately take me to Bergen Pines, which had opened in 1916 as a hospital for patients with tuberculosis and other contagious diseases. Now, it was addressing the worst contagion of all: drug addiction.

We met with an intake person. I told her that my schedule involved running the business that I hated by day and then (newly out of the closet) running out to gay bars and discos by night, and that I'd had to drop out of college to be this miserable. The intake person listened as my story tumbled out of me, sounding even worse than I thought. Then she turned to Rita and said, "It's clear to me that your brother needs a break. The contrasting lifestyles create internal havoc that is detrimental to his long-term mental health."

Hearing those words out loud was so freeing. At last someone had confirmed what I knew deep down in my heart. I needed someone else to tell my family because family guilt had brought me to this point. I needed Rita, who was not benefiting from my working in the business, to help me get out of the business so I could hold on to whatever sanity I had left.

With tears streaming down my cheeks, my chin on my chest, and my eyes closed, I could not contain my despair and I started to shake. I was ashamed because I felt weak. I had known change was imminent because I was beginning to feel like there was nothing left for me to live for. I didn't want to check into Bergen Pines because of the stigma that came with it. I wanted to avoid having all the town yentas "tsk-tsk-ing" upon hearing the news. God forbid I bring shame to my mother.

Back then, addicts were committed to mental institutions because Betty Ford hadn't yet gotten addicted to pain killers, which paved the way for rehabs to become the new black.

I wanted to get away from everything I knew and breathe new air. The next best thing was to head west, put a hundred down, and buy a car, in a week, maybe two… We'll see how that works out. I had always dreamed of Hollywood. I thought about the infamous sign where a wannabe actress, Peg Entwistle, had leaped to her death in her bid for fame. If I were to stay in Secaucus and jump off the roof of my single-level warehouse because I felt like a failure and life was not worth living, as Peg had, maybe I'd end up with a broken leg or arm. All roads led me out of Dodge. I knew I had to leave.

During one of our midnight chats, I finally found the gumption to tell my mother that I was leaving the company and going to California for a while. The conversation had started, as usual, with us reflecting on the day and complaining. Finally, I spilled my guts to her. I was doing Tom Joad in the final scene of what I'd call my *Grapes of Wrath* moment:

"I have to leave, Maw."

"What do you mean? Where are you gonna go?"

Outer-bum-fuck sounded like a good idea, I wanted to say. "I don't know, Ma. Maybe I can do something. Find something that matters."

"What about work?"

"I don't know yet. I'll be everywhere. I'll be all around in the dark."

"I don't understand. What's the problem?" She knew I really had no business working at Sivar.

"Maybe I can just find something that matters. I can't live in this world."

"But you're making such good money."

"Money is not bringing me happiness. None of this matters to me. It's not my life. I mean…it's friggin' auto parts? This just ain't it."

"Where will you go?"

"California, I reckon."

"So far?"

"Yeah, Los Angeles, at least for a few weeks to think things through. I need to spread my wings. I need to see what's out there. I can't stay here, and what, this is it? Just making money? I'm only 21 years old. It will be the death of me." It would be the Death of an Auto Parts Salesman, for sure. The sound of that alone.

"I need to find what's out there. Something. Anything. I won't survive suburbia."

My mother was naturally concerned but loved me enough not to harp on why I needed to stay in a place of misery. I didn't need her to know how deeply troubled I was and what the psychologist had said. I tried to keep harsh truths from her. We all did that instinctively so as not to upset or worry her. She'd had a hard enough life; we were always unwilling to cause undue stress.

I bought a one-way ticket to LAX, told Seymour I was done with Sivar once and for all, and wished him luck. On the flight, I sat next to a beautiful model/actress who initially ignored me, but by the time we were flying over Ohio, she started getting off on a Quaalude. Lord knows I could recognize that sexy slur a mile away. She offered me one, and by the time we landed, we were making out because, remember, Ludes did that to people, gender be damned. I rented a white Mustang convertible and drove up La Cienega Blvd until it ended at Sunset Boulevard. The top of La Cienega is a very steep hill, and since I had rented a stick shift, don't ask how uncool I was trying to turn onto Sunset Boulevard. Cringing, I finally made a right turn, and within a few blocks, I saw the Sunset Hotel and checked in. I walked around the neighborhood in awe of the infamous billboards and the people who seemed much more relaxed than New Yorkers. As a joke, I tried to get discovered at Schwab's, where legend has it that Lana Turner was discovered while sitting at the soda fountain. I sidled up to the counter and ordered a Coca-Cola…and *bubkes*.

I went to the Polo Lounge at the Beverly Hills Hotel for lunch the next day. This was back when everyone who was anyone was there to be seen. When the most powerful anyones like Swifty Lazar, Sue Mengers, or Freddie Fields got phone calls, the maître d' brought a vintage-style telephone to their table. Before I sat down, I called my sister Rita and told her to page me in fifteen minutes. Naturally, I was never paged because the maître d' knew who I was not. I called Rita after my meal and thanked her for trying. She said she wanted to come out to LA to make sure I was okay. Since Rita had been so supportive of my need to flee New Jersey and auto parts, I bought her a plane ticket so she could enjoy some fun in the sun. It was the least I could do to repay her kindness.

I picked her up from the airport a week later, and the first thing she said was "Guess whose parents are Holocaust survivors?"

"Us?"

"No, no, no, someone famous."

After I'd offered a few wrong guesses, she chimed in with "Henry Winkler."

In the late '70s, *Happy Days* was one of the most beloved television shows in the U.S. The cast was wildly popular, starting with Fonzie. The Fonz, played by Henry Winkler, was a goombah Johnnie—a greaser, Guido type, clad in a leather biker jacket. When Rita found out that Henry Winkler was Jewish and the son of Holocaust survivors, she went all-in on a plan to catch the tiger by the toe.

"I gotta meet him and tell him we have something in common. And you never know."

"You never know what, exactly?" I asked.

"Well, I'm sure if Holocaust parents raised him then all this Hollywood crap is making him want to settle down with a nice Jewish girl. Let's go to a taping of *Happy Days*. I'll get us tickets."

Rita had stars in her eyes; if anyone could pull off a miracle, it was my sister. After all, it was P.O.R. (Power of Rita) that had got us whisked into Studio 54 that first night.

Happy Days was corny American television. The other characters were Richie Cunningham, his pals Potsie and Ralph, Richie's little sister Joanie, and Chachi, her boyfriend. (Those two were filming a spin-off, *Joanie Loves Chachi*.)

Sure enough, Rita finagled VIP tickets to a taping at Universal Studios, and off we went, making a pit stop at Canter's Bakery on Fairfax Avenue to get *rugelach*. Rita was old-school and figured the way to even a celebrity man's heart was through his stomach. She maneuvered to get great seats and scoped out where we could do a meet-and-greet autograph moment. Someone sitting behind us was talking about Fonzie's real-life girlfriend, who was apparently remarkably plain-looking, and the fact that they had recently become engaged. That did not deter my sister. She figured if it wasn't a marriage yet, there was still a chance.

After the show's taping, Rita eagerly awaited her moment, standing with a group of aggressive Fonzie fans, white bakery box tied with red-and-white string in hand. She couldn't quite get close enough to connect, but I heard her throw out the word *Holocaust*.

The atmosphere was too hectic, and she couldn't get his attention. I thought she would surely throw a couple of *rugelach* at him, like tossing peanuts to a monkey at the zoo. Something, anything. The moment was slipping away. He noticed her but didn't respond. Rita went from being disappointed to annoyed in one fell swoop.

"Let's get out of here," she said.

We decided to use the bathrooms before we exited the studio. I waited a few minutes for Rita, who came out with a look on her face that said something terrible had just happened.

"What's the matter?"

"Ucchh, Joanie took a shit."

And just like that, we left Universal Studios, Rita's high hopes of becoming Mrs. Fonzarelli had been dashed by some other Jewish American Princess (J.A.P.) who landed the big fish. She opened the box, and we shared the *rugelach* in silence on the ride back to the hotel.

MAN-MADE

Remember the film *Perfect*, where Jamie Lee Curtis and John Travolta aerobicized themselves into living happily ever after? During the early '80s, Jane Fonda had become a fitness phenom, and Olivia Newton John's "Let's Get Physical" changed the landscape of MTV music videos, creating a hot new commodity. The sexy shorts that Studio 54 busboys wore became the look, and who didn't want to appear that desirable? The fitness industry was booming, which made daylife the desired lifestyle. AIDS had destroyed nightlife; it was cool to be out and about during the day, but you had to look good. Suddenly, health and wellness became the new black, and a membership to Gold's Gym Venice was the new "only" place to be seen. As soon as I landed back in NY, it was hard not to notice that the LA fitness lifestyle hadn't made it here yet.

I've never gotten involved in athletic pursuits after a life of body-shaming by myself and by others. There was only one sport I excelled in: partying. Chasing dealers for a high wasn't aerobic, and it was the worst kind of treadmill to be on. One night in Chelsea, I noticed a sign for Better Bodies Gym for Women directly above the gay bar

I frequented, Private Eyes. Now, there's a novel idea: working your pecs upstairs and downstairs, simply replacing dumbbells with cocktails. Talk about killing two birds with one (Sharon) stone!

After weeks of contemplation and two shots of Jägermeister at a happy hour, I ventured upstairs to inquire about getting butch alongside a gaggle of women. A beautiful Latina, Kelly, greeted me from the makeshift check-in counter. I checked out what would soon become my home away from home. I was surprised to see several stunning male creatures working out among the lesbians and began to feel my biceps curling. Something was tingling, anyway. Joining Better Bodies was a seminal moment; to this day, I have maintained fitness as an integral part of my life. Kelly hooked me up with a trainer, a big doofus named Johnny with an astonishing face and a bubble butt to match. I knew I was in the right place and wanted to be a brick shithouse like the other guys and girls who worked out there. I began replacing my other addictions with endorphin rushes, making this new workout lifestyle a six-day-a-week habit. And, like God, I rested on the seventh day.

Training with Johnny over several months transformed my body and led me to consider that I could do this for a living. The fashionista crowd I had been spending time with wasn't known for their healthy lifestyles. In fact, they pooh-poohed those who replaced vodka with green juices. Their flighty pursuits were vapid and uninteresting, and their attitudes made me think, "Can you remove your label so I can see right through you?" Fashionistas were more impressed with hookers than with those of us who were striving to live a cleaner lifestyle. I contemplated a career as a fitness trainer because it was a better way of life, and legitimate jobs were starting to emerge. (Although hookers are still the rage and perhaps always will be, now we call them influencers.) Jewish boys weren't the traditional hooker type. I tried it once, with catastrophic results.

A guy who frequented Better Bodies struck up a conversation with me and mentioned that he worked at a male escort service procuring "talent." After he'd invited me several times to come in for an interview, I thought, "What do I have to lose? Surely not my virginity." He handed me a black card with only a phone number. When I called the number, I laughed when I heard the name of the company: "Man-Made." So fitting. I arranged to go in for an interview and arrived at a seedy office building in the heart of the garment center, which also made sense. I rode up the rickety elevator and stepped into the Man-Made offices, which could have easily been some kind of Mafia payola front. The hooker booker, a skinny, smoking, older queen, looked me up and down.

"Take off your shirt," he said.

I did so with utmost confidence. He got up, walked over to me, touched my biceps with one hand, grabbed my crotch with the other, and said, "You'll do." He picked up his Polaroid camera and took two photos.

"Don't call us, we'll call you," the hooker booker said.

A week later, while getting ready to go out, I got "the call" — the callboy call, as it were. Had I walked out the door one minute earlier, it would have been a missed opportunity. I refused to wear a beeper, as the hooker booker had suggested, because it interrupted my silhouette in the same way that a fanny pack or a colostomy bag would. The hooker booker told me to go to the New York Hilton Hotel to "escort" a VIP to dinner.

"You mean all I have to do is go to dinner with this guy, and he'll give me three hundred dollars?"

"Yup. You will have to escort him back to the hotel."

Lesson One in being a hooker: Read between the lines of what your hooker booker says. If something sounds too good to be true, it probably is.

Lesson Two: The word *escort* means poontang.

Zooming over to the Hilton, I met my extremely short "date" in the lobby.

"Oy." *Sotto voce.*

He turned out to be the Ambassador to Somewhere.

I suggested we dine at Chanterelle, a Michelin 3-star restaurant a short walk away on Fifth Avenue. Dinner was delicious, as were the cocktails, but the conversation somewhat stilted.

"To what country are you the Ambassador?"

"I'm not at liberty to discuss."

"Um, but what does an ambassador do?" I wanted to know and wanted him to do all the talking about himself because powerful men love that, and this would allow me to eat and drink while nodding with feigned interest.

He was devoid of personality; his short answers forced me to ask more questions.

"What's your favorite movie?" I asked after a long silence, attempting to restart the conversation.

"*The Bridge on the River Kwai.*"

"Mine is *How to Marry a Millionaire.*" It was a lie because *The Wizard of Oz* was my favorite movie, but I thought the Marilyn Monroe moment was a better line, given the situation. That was the high point of the dinner conversation, which finally ebbed to silence. We walked back to the Hilton as a light drizzle began to fall for an added annoying effect.

The ambassador said that his cash was in the safe upstairs in the suite and to please join him to retrieve the fee and a nightcap. Eager for the cash and never one to refuse a nightcap, I rode up the 47 floors to the massive suite. I'd never seen such luxury: floor-to-ceiling windows overlooking Central Park and the twinkling lights of Manhattan. If Dorothy thought she wasn't in Kansas, I definitely wasn't at the Stevensville Hotel at Swan Lake in the Catskills.

The ambassador went into the bedroom and came out totally nude, sporting a two-inch penis.

"What are you doing?" I asked, horrified at the size of his manhood.

"What do you mean? You're my dessert."

"But we just had profiteroles. This was not part of the deal. I was told to escort you to dinner."

"What do you think *escort* means?" he asked, raising his voice.

There was no way I was putting out to this guy. I'm not some hooker with a heart of gold.

I was livid and not doing a thing without cash in hand first. I stood by the door.

"I need to call Man-Made. Can I please use your phone?"

The rude while nude ambassador approached me in all his tiny undesirableness. I would say he was trying to cock-block me, although that wouldn't apply here. He started massaging my chest with all the finesse of Frankenstein's monster. There was no way I could close my eyes and hold my breath through this encounter. Fortunately, the phone rang. Saved by the bell! The undignified dignitary answered the call, stuttering.

"Yes, I see. Well, well, well, I was just getting into bed."

Brech, which is *vomit* in Yiddish.

"Very well, I'll be down in a minute," he said, giving me the evil eye. "Lucky for you, my colleagues are downstairs and want me to join them for a drink."

"What a shame. My cash, please?" Not skipping a beat.

He scurried like a rat back to the bedroom and returned with a wad of bills, peeling off three crisp hundreds.

"Yeah, no taxi driver is going to break a hundred." I felt like Jane Fonda in *Klute*.

He peeled off a twenty and threw it at me, and I scampered out of the suite, vowing to be a good Jew and never hustle again. Not this kind, anyway.

"So that happened," I said to my reflection in the elevator mirror on the long ride to the lobby, snickering at what had just happened. I stepped outside and noticed that the rain had stopped. I looked at the sky or God and asked, "What was I thinking?" With the dosh in my pocket, I sashayed over to my drug dealer's apartment, bought an eight-ball of blow, and headed downtown to Boy Bar in the East Village.

Reflecting on the evening, I was no longer snickering at what had transpired; rather, I was disappointed that this was something I had allowed myself to entertain. Who cares how much people welcome hookers into their fold? I was the son of two warriors who had sacrificed so much to give me a good life, and here I was, pissing it all away. My decision-making prowess needed a refresher course. I snuck a couple of bumps in the cab, and the drizzle started again. The sound of the monotonous windshield wipers annoyed me and reminded me of the metronome on Vivian's upright piano when she was a student at Julliard.

I stepped into the rain on St. Mark's Street and walked into the dark, loud bar. I noticed my friend Sal and motioned him to follow me into the bathroom to share our vials of accouterment. Not even asking what he was shoving up my nose, I started feeling really woozy. The combination was not optimal, and drinking shots of Jägermeister along with a Jack and Coca-Cola didn't make things any clearer. The next thing I knew, I was barfing up the contents of my stomach in the dirty, dark bathroom, living up to the expression "hugging the toilet." Sal put me in a cab and gave the driver my address, as I had nodded out.

The driver tapped on my knee from the front seat.

"Hey, buddy, you're here."

I groggily paid the man, fumbled with my keys, and, with one eye closed, put the key in the lock and made my way to bed. The room was spinning, and I swore that this was the last time, which is what I had said the last time and the time before that. I was sick and tired of hearing myself say "Never Again." Holocaust aside, and I mean no disrespect, but clearly, I needed to be freed from the bondage of self. Could I or would I ever get off this catastrophic merry-go-round?

SAN MIGUEL DE ALLENDE:
FROM DISCOS TO FRESCOS

omehow, a decade went by, and I woke up from a stupor in a duplex penthouse in Gramercy Park. The building was a renovated warehouse on East 23rd Street that I had lucked into through a lost, first-love romance. Long story, not for now. The rent was reasonable, considering it had eighteen-foot ceilings, ten-foot wall-to-wall windows, and a two-tiered sun deck, which was the roof of the entire building. I had every inch of the place painted white since the sky was my view. I remember one party where 250 people attended, and it never felt crowded. It isn't important now to know what and when and how and where and with whom I managed to live this well while high; the more important fact is that I wanted to end the misery that came with the lifestyle. It felt like I was trying to drive in the fast lane in a car with no gas.

Hungover, as usual, I found myself wandering the streets of New York City, walking aimlessly from my apartment and winding up in Greenwich Village at the Christopher Street Pier. I loved to watch the kids who'd come downtown from Harlem to have Voguing dance-offs to rehearse for the next uptown drag ball. The Kiki Culture was raging and was the inspiration for Madonna's greatest hit, "Vogue." I gazed beyond them, despondently, at the unimpressive New Jersey skyline. The castle-shaped tower in Weehawken reminded me of the antisemitism and low-rent neighbors we had moved on up from. Things had gotten so bad that the thought of going home to Mother seemed like a viable option to get off the not-so-merry-go-round.

The blustery cold winter wind that wafted off the Hudson River slapped my face and snapped me out of that mindset, thank God, I mean, goodness. I skulked through the West Village in search of a café where I could warm up. I stumbled upon a dark, smoky place whose name escapes me; actually, it was the No Name Café on Hudson Street. The name fit the mood.

A rare Gruyère cheeseburger with bacon and a mound of well-done French fries called my name. Comfort food. I needed a dose of what food had always given me when I was a fat kid: nurturing, healing, soothing, making me feel whole. The waiter approached, and I opted for coffee, which had brought me to the No Name Café in the first place. It was just after 5 PM, and the 9-to-5 workers were scurrying home to the silence of their small West Village apartments that they were thrilled to have. I gazed at the passersby. People-watching had become one of the few sports I'd mastered. I often fantasize about how much fun it would be to set up a table on any random street corner in New York City, á la Lucy from the *Peanuts* comic strip, but instead of "Psychiatric Help," I would dispense "Style Help, The Doctor Is ALWAYS In." It astounded me how many New Yorkers looked so unstylish as well as miserable as they hustled from their high-pressure day jobs to their small apartments, trapped inside their heads, never looking up, deep in thought. I wondered if, like me, they were thinking about how lonely their lives in the Big Apple really were, wondering whether their lives would be better lived in the small towns from which they came. It was easier to think about what troubled other people than to figure out how to fix my own life.

Are you one of those people who love to eavesdrop on other people's conversations (OPC) while dining out at restaurants? I sure am, craning my neck ever so slightly to switch the superpower hearing on and off in an effort to catch conversations at nearby tables. The trick is to swallow hard, like when you're on an airplane as it descends to land, clearing the ear canals that serve as the dial tuning into a channel so you can hear everything being said. Anything was better than listening to what was going on inside my own head. I'd spent my entire childhood browbeating myself for being over-weight and not having the determination to love myself enough to stop eating until I did. That didn't mean I actually loved myself yet. Rather, I just didn't hate myself as much anymore. Allowing myself to do the amount of drugs I was doing proved that I still had a long way to go to find self-love.

The chic, striking, blonde woman sitting next to me reminded me of one of my Studio 54 club kid drug buddies, with her Coupe Sauvage haircut, perfectly worn-out black leather jacket, and lots of chunky silver jewelry. Her look intrigued me, and I wanted to hear what she and her otherwise unexceptional-looking friend were chatting about. The friend was wearing a plaid, flannel shirt with shoulder pads, stonewashed jeans, and a ponytail held together with a Scrunchie. I questioned what these two could possibly have in common.

We're taught, "Don't judge a book by its cover." Then again, since I was a recent refugee from the fashion industry, all I did was judge. The books, the shelves they sat on, the homes the shelves were in, the way the owners of the shelves dressed, what cars they drove…it was insidious. Frankly, I was over it. Next! I successfully tuned into the ladies' conversation, turning up the volume dial in my brain.

"How's the book coming along?" Plain Jane asked the blonde. Of course, the woman I'm obsessed with is writing a book. No doubt some fabulous roman á clef based on her life of fabulousness.

"Please, I haven't scratched out a paragraph in months," she lamented and began ruminating about the ills of New York City, not being able to get in touch with her creative spirit, suffering from writer's block. As the conversation progressed, I gleaned that Miss Fabulosity wasn't so fabulous after all. Of course, she needed to say that she was writing a book. It made her sound interesting to her friend, who turned out to be the interesting one. The blonde may have been wearing a Claude Montana jacket, but that didn't make up for her feelings of inadequacy as she droned on about her chaotic relationships with men who were unwilling to commit and how much she hated her 9-to-5 job at an art gallery where no one ever walked in. She was one of those garden-variety New Yorkers who wasn't truly happy living in the concrete jungle. Rather, like caged animals, they're conditioned to stay in their newfound habitat and act as if their lives mattered.

As it turned out, Miss Jane was not so plain, but the fiercer one; a writer who actually wrote, whose first book had been on *The New York Times* Bestseller List and whose articles had been published in *Harper's Bazaar*. She rifled through her Birkin bag, pulled out a Chanel lipstick and compact, and reapplied. She was prettier than I'd realized.

"Have you ever been to San Miguel de Allende?" the prolific writer asked the pretty, sad soul.

"No, Sheila, where is it?"

Where was this San whatever-she-just-said, I wondered, discreetly holding my nose and forcing more air from my ears to hear what they were saying more clearly.

"It is in a remote part of Mexico," Sheila answered. "God's country, my go-to place when I'm experiencing writer's block. I don't tell many people about San Miguel. It's still untouched in many ways."

"Really?" we both asked, the blonde aloud, me in my head.

Sheila continued describing what sounded like heaven until I was hanging onto her every word.

"It's an ancient Spanish Colonial city that was settled by the Christians in the 1500s to promote Christianity. There are literally dozens of magnificent churches, cobblestone streets, stunning hand-painted tiles from Dolores Hidalgo, beautiful architecture, these grand walled-off homes with courtyards. It's where artists go to recharge and study because there are three art schools there. People come from all over the world. Well, it's just amazing. The people are incredible, and the food…"

The blonde wanted to believe her. "But what if I don't know what I really want to do with my life? Will being there help me figure that out?" she pleaded.

"All I can say is that if it doesn't, you'll at least get the clarity to figure out what it is you *don't* want, and that's half the battle if you ask me," Sheila offered. "Just go. It's incredible. After two weeks, I get rejuvenated and am able to write shitloads of fresh stuff, which I am now finishing up for my publisher."

The blonde hesitated. "I don't know; it seems like a frivolous thing to do. And what do I tell my boss? As it is, I've used up all my sick days and have taken my vacation days to nurse hangovers."

"Excuse me," I interrupted, boldly leaning into their private conversation. "Can you please spell that? Pardon me for eavesdropping, but San what-was-that?" I blurted out, almost falling off my chair. Rather than giving me the typical New Yorker response with attitude, Sheila smiled brightly at me. She had found someone who was interested in taking her sage advice.

"San Miguel de Allende. It's a tiny village deep in the Sierra Madre Mountains of Mexico. It's a 500-year-old city, completely preserved. Not a lot of Americans; it's like heaven on Earth," she explained.

"Again, pardon the intrusion; it just sounds so lovely," I said. The blonde fidgeted in her seat. As I began to return to my cup of coffee, Sheila asked me to join them. At that moment, I was convinced that this was God stepping in to say, "Trust the process." Making eye contact with the blonde, I said, "If that's okay with you." Even if it wasn't.

"Of course. Maybe I could be convinced to go to San Miguel with a little support," the blonde said. I pulled my chair around with one hand and grabbed my coffee in the other. The waiter walked by and gave us a look that implied more about sexual innuendo than the innocent conversation we were having about a place that could potentially be the answer to all my problems. Could such a place really exist? Since Sheila had already convinced me that it did, I wasn't going to argue; rather, I was ready to pack a bag and get the hell out of Dodge. I was already feeling better just from hatching a plan in my head.

Sheila's energy was a great antidote to my despondency; I wanted to be her. Next stop: San Miguel de Allende. Maybe I would try my hand at becoming a writer. As the old adage goes, "Write what you know." Perhaps I had a Jacqueline Susann-type sexcapade novel in my head. Who doesn't love a good, juicy beach read? The blonde, whose name was Diana, was almost convinced to take the leap of faith, but I could tell from her hesitation that she would never do it. She was one of those New Yorkers who were stuck in their ruts and couldn't find their way out. I thanked the girls for the gift and welcomed the night air as I walked with newfound enthusiasm to the Christopher Street subway station to catch the next train home. Fuck it, I hailed a Checker cab, because at this point every moment counted, and I couldn't afford the luxury of wandering.

The next morning, I booked a month-long trip to San Miguel de Allende. Surely, maybe, hopefully that would be more than enough time to jot down my "novel" novel. I ran to Crazy Eddie's, the well-televised appliance store with that obnoxious yelling pitchman, and purchased a cumbersome word processor. I was initially planning to buy a Smith-Corona typewriter like the ones so many famous authors had used. But when I confessed that I had never been a great typist, the saleswoman convinced me that word processors were the wave of the future and computers were just for geeks.

I schlepped the gargantuan box home and assessed my planned haul to San Miguel de Allende: a box the size of a minibar and two *jagunza* pieces of luggage. The weather in Mexico was going to be great; anything would be better than a New York winter.

The car service picked me up on a snowy Sunday morning. Fifty shades of gray was the sky's color scheme, and the promise of sunshine and green mountaintops loomed on the horizon. The driver was about the age that my father would have been, and he had a heavy Jewish accent like Dad did. I looked out the window at the quiet Sunday-morning Manhattan streets and started a conversation with him, hoping it would be like communicating with my dad. Oddly enough, it was. He thought my journey sounded exciting and was supportive in a way my family could never manage to be. When I called them to say *hasta luego*, they asked all the wrong questions. They were safely cocooned within their little lives and could not understand my need to spread my wings in yet another daring attempt to fly. The driver had moved to America in search of a good life, and, in his own way, he had found one. Driving people around would never have sufficed for me, but I wasn't going to be my usual self, quick to sit in judgment. Instead, we talked about his work. He enthusiastically told me about the time Barbra Streisand was in his cab, and he said that she was an angel, unlike her reputation. I was glad to hear this because she was one of my heroes, and if I'm being honest, I consider myself a funny girl.

Contrary to warnings, AeroMexico was a great airline. You know how naysayers have a way of popping out of the woodwork the moment you book a trip? Shopkeepers, One Hour Martinizers, acquaintances—they're all the same. Everyone is a travel expert. Granted, I could have done without the Mariachi music piped through the loudspeaker from boarding till takeoff. Otherwise, the flight to Mexico City couldn't have been more pleasant. The smart outfits the air hostesses wore were lovely, and the Mexican airplane food was far above just barely edible. I sat near two sophisticated women from Mexico City who spoke fluent English. They were both in their mid-thirties and had come to New York to attend as many photography exhibits and galleries as possible because they wanted to become photographers. Ladies who *lonchería*. Our conversations centered on the fashion and beauty industries that were the center of my existence, and the five-hour flight whizzed by.

The Mexican immigration and customs crew scared the living daylights out of me. First of all, as I approached the immigration counter, lugging my luggage and kicking along the cow-patterned word processor box, the short, pie-faced, dark-haired man looked at me in disgust, grunted, and didn't stamp my passport.

"Scuzee," I muttered to Señor Sour Puss, "Yu no stampa la passport para mi."

He looked at me with glazed eyes; he'd seen one too many gringos that day. He mumbled at me to keep the line moving, so I folded my passport and kept going. How was I going to prove to everyone that I was abroad instead of hiding out in New Jersey? At the moment, I had no real proof that I was hiding out in Mexico. The more pressing challenge presented itself shortly thereafter: trying to explain to the Customs agent—another short, pie-faced person—that my sole purpose for coming to Mexico was NOT to sell my word processor. The Customs agent knew enough English to tell me that I had to pay some ridiculous duty fee for my newfound accessory.

"Scuzee, señnorita," I tried to sweet talk my way out of paying the exorbitant fine. "Es mi writing thing," I smiled.

Señorita Sour Puss was lip-syncing to Selena and could barely hear me. She yelled in a heavy accent that she wanted 300 U.S. dollars, which I imagined would go directly into her pocket. At the same time, the photographers were snagged trying to bring in Persian throw rugs in their luggage and pass them off as old ponchos. The now-exasperated Señorita Sour Puss was not having any of us. She was accustomed to Customs scammers, and the three of us were just pissing her off.

Fortunately, the two lovely wanna-be photographers' husbands had arrived to greet them at the airport. They assessed the situation and worked their charm on the señorita. These handsome, chivalrous men had come to our rescue. One told the Customs agent in fluent Spanish that his wife was insane and that she had just come from "a rest" in a U.S. mental institution. He then explained to Señorita Sour Puss that I was a writer doing a story on her life and needed my machine to write it. He was quick on his feet, and the story was so far-fetched it almost seemed plausible to me. It was also the first time I had been referred to as a writer, and I liked the way it sounded.

The photographers, their husbands, and I said our goodbyes at the bus depot where I was bound for San Miguel. Somehow, when I was making my plans I had not realized that the ride to San Miguel was five hours northwest into the Sierra Madres. I could have sworn it was a suburb of Mexico City. Where the fuck was Google when you needed it? Oh, not invented yet. Still within earshot, one of the husbands came to my rescue and explained to me that I had missed the only daily express bus to San Miguel, which took three hours, and that the local bus was leaving in ten minutes. Next stop, paradise.

The bus was filled with migrant workers, people transporting live chickens, and me with a box the size of a mini-bar on my lap. At one point, a woman with two children and a pig boarded the bus and they sat motionless, wordless, till they got off at a stop before San Miguel. As our bus trekked up the endless range of mountains toward our final destination, a huge stone statue named Conin appeared like a mirage. He was a native Mexican who had helped the Spaniards conquer the territories of Mexico to usher in Christianity. Sounds barbaric.

The bus puttered up the hill, navigated yet another treacherous bend, and then we finally began our descent into the valley where San Miguel de Allende was comfortably nestled. The sun was setting over the darkening purple Sierra Madre Mountains as we pulled up to what might be called a bus depot, but which looked more like a hut. My immediate concern was getting all my crap to wherever the fuck I was going next. I had been so consumed with getting here and becoming a famous writer that I hadn't considered where I would stay for the night, much less the next month. Call it bad planning or spontaneity, it contributed to the adventure. The bus driver helped me unload my stuff on the roadside. I gave him five dollars, and his face lit up with a smile that made me realize how nice it is to be appreciated for the littlest things. Then again, five American dollars back then was like 500 dollars is today, and when you transfer that into pesos, he could have retired.

Standing in the dark night, I saw a beam of light coming toward me, and like a Christmas miracle, a beat-up Toyota Corolla putt-putted up and a smiling man hopped out.

"Habla Inglés?" I gestured with my hands.

"Si," he replied.

"Hotel para mi?" I asked.

"Si," he replied.

Well, now, that could have been taken any of a number of ways, but I started putting my stuff in his car and hopped in the front to be personable. We sat in silence for a brief moment, and I repeated, "Hotel para mi, por favor?"

"Las Monjas esta muy bueno," he replied.

"Ya," I said, realizing that it sounded less Spanish and more Swedish.

"Las Monjas mucho gusta," he said.

Off we went in the dark to what I was truly hoping was a hotel. Through the cobblestone streets we bounced till we arrived at an old, red Spanish-Colonial-style building. I paid the man, took my stuff into this odd but beautiful building where no one was present, and called out "Hola," pleased that I'd retained some key words from my high school Spanish classes. I couldn't remember the Spanish words for *bath* or *bed*, but I knew somehow I would improvise. A sweet little lady appeared through a wooden door behind the front desk. In even more fractured Spanish, I inquired about renting a room, although it looked more like we were playing charades. Within minutes, I was in a room, humble as it was, where I undressed and ran a bath. The long day's journey into night was over, and I felt invigorated and wanted to walk around and explore my new surroundings. I bathed, changed clothes, and went outside.

The town square was a hop, skip, and jump away from Las Monjas. There was some sort of floral festival going on, and the square was filled with countless vendors of the most amazing flowers I had ever seen, in colors that I'd never known to exist. It was like Alice sans looking glass or acid. I heard a few teenagers speaking English and moved slowly toward them, trying to make eye contact. They were having a grand old time frolicking amid the splendor of the flowers.

"Amazing, isn't it?" I asked. "I've never seen anything quite like this in my life."

Smiling warmly, one of the teens, a chubby, bubbly girl, agreed instantly. Before long, we were talking about where we were from and why we had come to San Miguel. As luck would have it, the friendly teenagers were also staying at Los Monjas. They were exchange students from the Chicago Institute of Art and the Rhode Island School of Design (RISD), attending Institute Allende, one of the three art schools Sheila had mentioned. After strolling around the square, we meandered back to the hotel, which was apparently the only evening activity in San Miguel—meandering, that is. We talked for what seemed like hours, and I was amazed that part of my brain was still working after years of being obliterated by fashion-related hullabaloo. I hadn't had an intelligent conversation since freshman year of college before I had dropped out to run my father's business. Not to mention the vapidity of the disco crowd that I ran with, where the only meaningful conversations were restricted to what libations were on tap for the evening. The ease of getting back on my verbal horse was gratifying proof that I hadn't killed every last brain cell. We sauntered (another San Miguel pastime) along the cobblestone streets and arrived at the hotel. The kids told me that Las Monjas had originally been a monastery. It seemed that this was God's country after all, though I'd rejected his existence after my father's death. Yet another old adage came to mind: "Never say never."

We sat on the veranda as tiny twinkling lights flickered in the buildings surrounding the hotel. We talked through the night, and as the sun began to peek its tangerine head above the Sierra Madres, I excused myself and retreated to the room since it had been twenty-four hours since I'd departed from New York, and I was exhausted.

We'd had a great evening without sex, drugs, or rock 'n' roll. Not even tequila! I'd done more than enough of the above to last me a lifetime. Taking a break from all libations sounded like a sound idea. These happy teenagers were living their best lives, pursuing their art, traveling abroad to nurture their craft, talking about things that mattered. I'd become a slave to the rhythm of a lifestyle that was consumed with fashion, clubbing, and nothing that truly mattered. What had been the center of my existence was, in fact, merely banal. The smoke and mirrors that cloud the fast lane had turned this grounded, earth-sign, ex-Hippie into a self-congratulating victim of the "my shit don't stink" crowd. Ahhhh…perspective.

We said our goodnights, and I went up to my room. The limited renovations that had turned the original monastery into a hotel made me want to throw on a black habit, fold my arms into the bell sleeves, and sing "Ave Maria" in honor of my mother, followed by a medley from *The Sound of Music* because I was ready to climb every mountain. Was I the Maria in this situation whose problems needed to be solved? Don't answer that.

I sang, danced, and laughed in my room. The furniture consisted of a single bed and a huge cross hanging on the wall. I got on my knees and began saying the Lord's Prayer. It had been eons since I'd been solemn, and the act of prayer seemed appropriate and comforting.

Dear God,
Now I lay me down to sleep, I pray the Lord my soul should
keep. If I should die before I wake, don't you dare let that
happen! Goodnight.
Love,
ABE

*P.S. As you can see, it has been years since I considered you
part of my life after you decided to take my father before
I could, at least, apologize for what I said to him… instead of
giving him a long life, which he absolutely deserved. But now
that I am here in God's, I mean, your country, I am happy
to be reacquainted with you and am willing to believe that
you exist, or at the very least, I don't despise you anymore.
Goodnight.*
Love,
ABE

Becoming a writer would suit me just fine, but what would I write about? Did I have a distinct voice? Had I lived enough life to garner sufficient perspective and experience to jot down stories that people could relate to? Was I interesting and analytical enough? Would anyone want to publish my stories? In my head, I said no to all of the above. I fell into a deep sleep and woke up the next morning to the sound of church bells ringing. Since there are thirty-four churches in San Miguel, imagine that serenade. Had I died and gone to heaven? It was noon. I opened the shutters and took in the sensory overload of the crisp, fresh air and sweeping mountain views. From seemingly nowhere Enya's hauntingly beautiful chorus "Sail Away" could be heard. It was magical.

I was famished and needed *huevos rancheros, arroz con pollo*, and *fajitas* for breakfast. I jumped into a pair of khaki shorts and a T-shirt with the word "Loco" on it that I had purchased at a flea market years before; when I was packing, I knew it would be a big hit. As I walked into town, I was able to see just how glorious this village was. You would never know you were in the 20th century unless an occasional beat-up Chevy passed by. Donkeys were the vehicles of choice, and horses served as cop cars. Mexican blankets were everywhere, and I couldn't wait to buy a few. But first, I needed food.

Looking for a restaurant, I noticed a sign that said (in English) "Everyone's Welcome." I hadn't seen any English words since I left JFK. I peeked into the pink stone building and witnessed what felt like a ritual of some sort: people sitting in a circle, intensely listening to one of the group members who sobbed as he spoke. I couldn't hear what was going on, but this was not the welcoming sight that the sign had implied. On the contrary, my interest, although piqued, was not going to take me further into this environment. I was backing up slowly when, all of a sudden, a gray-haired woman in the circle turned and motioned for me to sit next to her in an empty chair. "Welcome, son," she said with a weird, wide smile.

"I thought this was a café; sorry to intrude." I turned and ran out the door and down the cobblestone street as though I'd seen a ghost. I stopped to catch my breath and found myself standing in front of an enormous church. I was drawn in and stood in the dark, cavernous space as the light from the stained-glass windows cast colorful patterns on my khaki shorts. I sat in a pew and noticed a few fat women kneeling on the other side of the aisle. They were so deep in meditation that they didn't even notice my arrival. Imagine being that deep in prayer. The only time I had been that unconscious was when I was actually unconscious from too much alcohol or drugs. I closed my eyes, took a few deep breaths, looked up at the altar, and tried to communicate with God. "Hail Mary?"

I lost track of time, left the church, and walked around San Miguel in awe of its historic, elaborate simplicity. I finally found a little café and sat at an outdoor table. A waiter groggily approached, and I ordered a coffee and *huevos rancheros*. I tilted my head up and closed my eyes to let the sun warm my face. If I was going to be a writer, a good tan would be important for the many interviews and book signings that lay ahead. A shadow covered my face, and I opened my eyes and was startled to see the gray-haired lady standing over me with that same weird smile.

"Why did you run off?'" she asked. "There's another one tonight at 6:30."

"Excuse me?" I said.

"There's another meeting tonight at 6:30," she repeated.

"I don't know what you're talking about. I'm just waiting for my breakfast."

"Breakfast at this hour? Well, you really should come to the meeting tonight. If you like, I can go with you."

"I don't..."

"Listen, kid, I might be old, but I ain't stupid." She sat down next to me. "Mind if I join you for a cup of coffee?"

"Uh, frankly..." I dreaded the inevitable, but I liked the "kid" reference.

"Thanks, don't mind if I do; my name is Lee."

She plopped down and began preaching about how wonderful life was now that she was sober and that I had made the first step by coming into the meeting. I couldn't get a word in edgewise, and it was really beginning to annoy me. At what point did she think I gave a damn about her years of alcohol abuse, the fact that her father was an alcoholic, and her history of going from one bad relationship to another, enabling her to drink to get drunk. It was enough to make me want to order a shot of tequila, but out of respect for the recovering elderly, I refrained. She asked me if I had read *Postcards from the Edge* by Carrie Fisher, which I hadn't because I was too busy taking drugs to sit down and read a book about taking drugs. Apparently, Carrie Fisher was the new guru of sobriety, and it was always good for the cause when a celebrity talked frankly about their addiction. I promised that I would see if there was a copy in town and read it right away. She whipped a copy of the book out of her bag and said, "Here, you can borrow mine, but give it back."

Breakfast came, and this gave her the opportunity to prattle on about her life, being sober, and the joy of having experienced a spiritual awakening. By the end of the meal, my frustration with Lee had diminished considerably, and I was happy to be conversing with her. She had long, elegant fingers, and I loved watching her reach for cigarette after cigarette, carefully placing them in her ivory holder and pontificating about her days in New York and LA. Hours went by, and we walked toward the town square as dusk set in.

Suddenly, hundreds of birds descended on the town square where the flower festival was in full bloom. I was confident that Lee, being a butch lesbian, would protect me. She laughed at how timidly I responded to the increasingly loud cacophony of birds singing, which she assured me was a nightly ritual that had existed for centuries. No one really knows why, but the birds come out to sing each night, and the townspeople congregate in awe to enjoy nature's choral orchestra. The hundreds of residents seemed so peaceful, enjoying the setting sun and the chirping of the birds. These Mexicans are not poor. They are rich with the wealth of this magical place, where everyone is smiling in the peaceful embrace of evening.

She went on to tell me about the home she had purchased a couple of years earlier for $12,000. She invited me to join her for dinner at her home: "Nothing fancy."

Off we went to her home, which I'd envisioned as a shack. We arrived at one of those walled-off Spanish Colonial masterpieces Sheila had mentioned at the No Name Café. We entered the ornate wooden door and stood in a huge courtyard with stunning hand-painted tiles. The house had several private entrances, somewhat U-shaped, leading to one huge common main room with a kitchen, dining, and living room. As we toured Lee's home, she mentioned that it was a lot of house for one person but loved knowing she owned something this beautiful compared to the many small apartments where she'd lived in New York City. We ended up in the main room where she prepared a simple dinner: a large salad, grilled avocado, rice, and beans with fresh tortillas, which were being spun all over town and sold in red-and-white checkered napkins. As we finished the lovely meal, Lee said, "You should live in that blue-tiled wing while you're here in San Miguel, Abe. I'll charge you forty dollars a week."

"That's ridiculous," I said.

"Sleep on it."

She walked me back to Las Monjas. The kids were outside chatting and met Lee. We talked for a while until I had to excuse myself and retire for the evening. Decisions, decisions. Live with an old lady or hang out with a bunch of kids. Not that being thirty-four was old, but living with a group of college kids did seem pointless. Besides, Lee was sober, and you-know-who could use a dose of sanity and sobriety. The sheer coincidence of Lee was yet another unexpected God shot, a term I would come to love, especially when they happened.

SIDE STEPPING

The next morning, I went to that AA meeting and told Lee that I'd be grateful to move into her place. Lee shared with the group that she was taking me under her wing. Everyone applauded, and for whatever reason, the film *Rosemary's Baby* and those odd neighbors came to mind. I was surrounded by well-wishers after the meeting, and several locals gave me their phone numbers, a signature move in AA. Trust issues abound; the program teaches you that in fact, kind people still exist. A group of us went for coffee after the meeting, another signature AA move, and we talked about being sober among all this tequila and the joys of serenity—a foreign concept and an art that needed to be mastered.

Lee helped me take my stuff from the hotel to her house. The kids were all in class, so I would catch up with them later. We walked up a cobblestone street, me teetering along carrying the cumbersome word processor and Lee lugging the rest. In the daytime, Lee's home was even more magical. Having my own wing in Casa de Fabulosity with a poetic view of the Sierra Madre Mountains was purely God working in my life. I set my space up, put my clothes away, and positioned the word processor so it faced the magnificent views of the mountains. Birds were chirping; I took a deep breath, closed my eyes, and, for the first time in a long while, I believed things were going to be okay. We went to a meeting and had dinner with the sweet, mostly American retirees. Now I had two communities to spend time with: the kids and the codgers. Lee suggested I keep a daily journal and just write whatever I was feeling—thoughts, memories—and take this time to connect with my creative spirit. What a blessing. She also suggested that by the third day I should start working on the Steps of AA and that she would serve as my temporary sponsor while I was in San Miguel.

"Great," I said, not knowing what that meant exactly.

Lee explained that she would help me navigate the emotional roller coaster ride of the early days of sobriety. That meant talking, reading from the Big Book, and sharing personal stories. You begin to understand how much you have denied doing what's in your best interest, and you learn how to not browbeat yourself. Now, that's a novel idea, literally. The Twelve Steps are a guide to being restored to sanity. Sobriety is a spiritual journey that can bring you to a place that feels wonderful. The thing is, I had to put a pin in using the word sanity for now. I wasn't ready to admit defeat nor accept having handed over my power to people, places, or things like drugs and alcohol.

The first three steps of AA are something I had to come to terms with and say out loud, not just think about. Admitting powerlessness over drugs and alcohol is the first step, and once you can admit that out loud, you have a shot at believing in a power greater than yourself. But it also says that we have to turn our will and our lives over to the care of God *as we understood Him.*

Dear God,

Remember me? Rumor has it that we're supposed to hang out,
BUT as to whether I'm gonna willingly turn my life over to
you, I'll let you know with a special telegram. I saw how well
you did with my dad. So, let's just take this one day at a time,
okay?
Love,
ABE

Once I had mastered the first three steps, my next challenge would be taking the dreaded fourth step, which is far more complicated because you put yourself under a microscope, look, and keep looking. Then you have to write down TMI about yourself, including bad habits, mistakes, lies, cheating, self-harm, and the overall nothing-good-you've-been-committed-to as a personal lifestyle choice. You think that sounds harsh? Try being the one who is guilty of all of the above.

SIDEBAR: Living with an AA sponsor is not for the faint of heart. Sometimes, just getting up for a midnight snack turned into a marathon Q & A session of unsolicited self-reflection. If Lee heard me tiptoeing to the kitchen, she would appear, cigarette in hand, brow furrowed, with nothing else to do. She always had a question that perhaps a therapist would ask, often veering in a direction that was a tad too personal for my liking, like that first night when she asked about my first sexual encounter.

"Well, if you must know, it wasn't until my senior year of high school. I was a really fat kid, and I lost a boatload of weight in my junior year of high school. The incentive was that my sister Vivian was getting married that upcoming September, which landed in the same week as starting my senior year of high school. I did not want to:

(A) Look like me anymore, and

(B) Show up to the wedding looking like me, either.

That's when I dropped a third of my body weight and got a girlfriend right away."

"Girlfriend?" Lee asked, knowing I was gay as a goose.

We both chuckled.

"Did you feel guilty at all?" Lee asked, which I thought was an odd question.

"Guilty? About what?"

"Well, if you knew you might be gay."

"Try growing up in a home that the Holocaust built. I have worked my whole life trying to deal with guilt—my guilt, my mom's, my dad's; it's an albatross that I needed to fling off. So no, I didn't feel guilty about not feeling guilty."

There were endless conversations that I needed to take a break from. It was almost like I had checked into rehab. I couldn't escape myself. The next morning, I went to visit the kids at Las Monjas who were heading off to a poetry writing workshop. They invited me along, and I sat in the back of the room and listened as students stood up to recite their assignments. I was inspired to try my hand at writing, and that night I sat at my word processor thinking about my life, the moment, and the many mistakes I had made.

IN SEARCH OF HAPPINESS POEM – Written at 1:00 am

We've all set out to conquer worlds,
*   Both known to us and new.*

And all of us suit up in armor,
*   But the ones who win are few.*

It's the chosen few I salute,
*   'Cause I've been one to lose.*

Then, sinking deep inside myself,
*   And cried and cried the blues.*

Until one day, I woke up,
*   And realized my battle was won.*

For I was here and still alive,
*   And saw there was much to be done.*

So, I set out on my new search,
*   Out of darkness into the day*
And realized all I needed was God,
*   And he would show me the way.*

Not that he would do my work,
*   For I knew it was up to me.*

Belief in God as spiritual growth,
*   Is what would set me free.*

Now I knew that I must seek happiness,
*   Which became a journey within.*

Dancing through time, mostly gone by,
*   To evaluate what was under this skin.*

I feared the fear I felt inside,
*   I cried 'cause I'd lost several years.*

And like a man who's lost his pride,
*   I shed a million tears.*

And so, I did, and the pain was lifted,
*   And I smiled with joy 'cause I'd been gifted.*

By a light that shone through the big dark cloud.
*   I was ready now to join the crowd.*

I realized now that I had reason,
*   To bask in the glory of my new season.*

All I had to do was take each day,
*   And live it well, so I could say*
That tomorrow is only going to be this great,
*   If I do today what I don't hate.*

The next morning, feeling good and creative, I went to the Instituto Allende and arranged to audit a few classes while I was in town. I loved that I could write a poem; whether it was good or not, I wouldn't know until someone heard it. In the meantime, I felt really great about the creative burst of energy. While I was at the Instituto, I saw a sign that said "POETRY READINGS — Thursday nights at Café Linda." I jotted down the address because that would be something I would definitely want to attend. I couldn't believe how joyous it felt to be in this strange and beautiful place—in just a matter of days, I had set up a comfortable life with good people, creativity, and good energy—nothing like my life in New York City, which I didn't miss. I was just gonna take it a day at a time and not be concerned about going back to New York or moving to Los Angeles. I was living in and for the moment. Lee had so many great stories about her time in LA, which is where she got sober. Making LA my final destination sounded like a good idea for my next step, especially now that my life was awash with steps.

One afternoon when I was at lunch with the kids, the conversation leaned into how they wanted to live their lives without regret. The question "What is your greatest fear?" was the topic, and the group was sharing. When it was my turn to speak, I said, "My greatest fear is that I don't have enough ambition that's required to fulfill my goals and dreams." That was a lot to hear myself say out loud. Why did I think this? Why had I been sabotaging myself all these years? Hence, addiction issues. This getting sober was getting way too real. My darkest, most fucked-up secret that I didn't even know I had was so close to the surface that it came spilling out of my mouth so effortlessly. Was I my own worst enemy? Here I thought I was the light, frothy, funny Abe, whereas deep down, there was a dark, vulnerable, defeated side of me that needed to be soothed and convinced that all was not lost and everything would be okay. The rest of the group's concerns were pretty astute; considering their ages, they had deep understandings of their internal worlds and what they wanted out of life, which made me ponder, "How vapid was I, and does that end now, or else?"

Later that night, at dinner, Lee and I had a long conversation about everything. She excused herself from the table and returned with a manilla folder that she said was a slew of questions her sponsor had used to help Lee claw through the Fourth Step when she got sober. She warned me that it was a series of very personal questions.

How much more personal can she get? I wondered. "I'm not so sure I'm ready to be interrogated," I said.

"I'll spare you what my sponsor put me through. That woman was a ball buster."

I looked at Lee with a cocked eye, acknowledging that she had become her master's apprentice.

"What painful memories do you have of your dad?" Lee asked.

Boom! I hated this already.

"Nothing like going for the jugular. Did you have to start with my Achilles heel?"

I told her about the time my dad was hospitalized with phlebitis, which the doctor said was a warning for him to slow down because he was such a butch workaholic. When I went to visit him in the hospital, it was out of character to see him lying there helpless and in pain. His discomfort made me uncomfortable. I went to the nurse's station and insisted they give him a Demerol shot, like that scene in *Terms of Endearment* when Shirley MacLaine freaks out when she sees her daughter, played by Debra Winger, wincing in pain. I had sat with my dad as he dozed off, wondering why we weren't close.

"That's sad," Lee said. "What about good memories?"

"To be honest, I don't have many. I remember asking my dad a few times to take me fishing in the summer on Swan Lake. Once, while he was playing poker with his buddies, he handed me a twenty-dollar bill and offered to have my Israeli uncle, who barely spoke English, take me. But I passed because fish be damned; it was my dad I wanted. Well, that never happened."

"That's a shame."

"Let me ask you something, Lee. Is spilling my guts gonna become a daily occurrence in this being-sober thing? Because I might need a drink or something."

Lee laughed and lit her umpteenth Marlboro Lite.

"What was your relationship with your dad?"

"As I said, not great."

"Did you resent him for that?"

"Resent? Hmmm. No, but I'm pissed that he died. Is that the same thing?"

"You tell me."

I was getting angry, remembering how awful the whole situation had been with him. The lack of closeness, feeling beyond guilty for what I had said that fateful day. I told Lee all the sordid details of his passing. I hadn't relived that nightmare in years.

"I thought I had processed all this already in therapy."

"Yes, but it sounds like you haven't forgiven yourself."

"All right, that's enough for one night." I was numb, but I actually felt glad to have gotten it off my chest.

"That's why we get sober—to grieve our pasts in order to move forward."

"Why? You don't think NOT dealing with things is a good idea?"

"Silly." She returned to her lair, leaving a cloud of cigarette smoke in her wake.

I went to my room and got on my knees to pray, which was something Lee suggested I do from time to time. It helps for some reason she couldn't explain.

The rest of my stay in San Miguel was like a beautiful dream. How blessed was I to have the confidence to follow the signs that seemingly appeared from nowhere, starting with the No Name Café, which seemed like a lifetime ago? All roads had led to this moment of clarity through this extended holiday in Mexico, which opened my heart and soul to a new possibility that my life could be different and better. With hope in my heart, I decided to move to Los Angeles. I had come to a dead end in New York City, with the operative word being *dead*, which thankfully wasn't me.

FIT FOR A QUEEN

Becoming a trainer was a natural progression for me. Yes, I said that. I had the patience of a saint and could count to fifteen. I crafted a bio that made me sound fearless, incorporating my fashion sense and experience while offering styling tips for clients needing a new wardrobe after losing all their excess weight. Like me, juice heads were thrilled to find a new career path for us high school and college dropouts. It was either this or being a bouncer at a nightclub, a security guard at a shopping mall, or a gym teacher.

> *Those who can, do. Those who can't,*
> *teach. Those who can't teach, teach gym.*
> *—Woody Allen, Annie Hall*

Next stop, Hollywood. Of all people, Richard Simmons was on board my flight to LA, which convinced me that if this *meiskeit* could make it in a business that's all about looks and persona, then I definitely had a shot. He was the Woody Allen of the fitness industry. He personified persona non grata because he was not hard to miss with that hairdo and all the screeching. His voice could break glass. Incredibly, Simmons was traveling with a bevy of handsome men who laughed at his every shrill. The best/worst moment was when he stood up, yanked an apron off the older gay flight attendant, and proceeded to serve water to several passengers, singing, "Fly the friendly skies of United." He approached me and bubbled, "Would you like to get wet?" I glanced up slowly from my *Vanity Fair*, barely smiled, raised my liter bottle of water, and shook my head no. Simmons then turned to a guy with a thick head of blond hair sitting across the aisle and asked, "Can I borrow your hair for a party I'm going to on Saturday night?" The blond barely acknowledged him as well. After Richard had passed us, I turned to the guy and said, "I won't have what she's having."

I drove around West Hollywood, amazed at all the FOR RENT signs and how easy it was to find a place to live. After spending several hours searching through perfectly acceptable dwellings, I settled on a furnished apartment in a neatly manicured complex, Mediterranean Village, complete with a swimming pool in the courtyard, smack dab in the middle of West Hollywood. When it was time to sign the lease, the building manager, Beatrice, an alcoholic-y-looking, cigarette-smoking, skinny, white-haired woman, looked at my application, then up at my face, and again at the application.

"Your name is Abe, huh?" she said in a tone with a hint of anti-Semitic disgust.

"As in Lincoln," I chirped, hoping she'd approve the application.

She looked up, snarled, scribbled on the application, and handed it back, countersigned with a set of keys.

"I'm just gonna call you Ace," she gurgled.

"Thank you so much, Beatrice."

As much as I, Abe, loved being christened with a non-Jewish name like Ace, I knew I'd never live up to it. I tried using it a couple of times when cruising the bars, thinking it might make me more desirable. On several occasions, I would scribble "ACE WAS HERE" with black marker on bathroom stalls, but that's as far as it went.

I moved my belongings into my apartment and joined Gold's Gym the same day. Watching these enormous knuckleheads, whose heroes were Arnold Schwarzenegger and Sylvester Stallone, push their workout partners to the limit helped me pick up a few tricks of the trade. It was a masterclass in bullshit. Besides, I had already mastered the most important attribute of being a good fitness trainer during my childhood. Fat boys know the importance of being a good listener to the pretty girls and helping them solve all their boy crush problems. This skill set was invaluable to ingratiating your clients. Besides, all you had to say to them during a one-hour session was "Uh huh, uh huh, right, uh huh, four, five, six, uh huh, uh huh, uh huh, thirteen, fourteen, fifteen, and rest. Great." The more intently you listened while thinking about what you were planning to have for lunch or that you needed to do laundry, nodding in agreement to whatever they were saying, the longer you kept the client.

The best thing about being a personal trainer in the late '80s was that you really didn't need any certification. You could fly by the seat of your pants, especially when that seat looked great in Spandex. Every celebrity, producer, director, spouse of, and wanna-be somebody was hiring personal trainers. "My Trainer" was the new must-have accessory du jour. We became the human "It Bag."

My first client was a heavy-set, mouth-breathing movie producer who had me come to his home in the Hollywood Hills—so high up in the hills that I worried that my Rent-A-Wreck might not make it. The house was a gated affair, and his wife, Shauna, was a rail-thin prototype for the Bravo *Real Housewives* franchise. Shauna opted out of our fitness sessions because she preferred Pilates and had a studio built overlooking the Olympic-sized pool. The Pilates instructor and I never fraternized because one thing you realize being a personal trainer is that your job is to be Listener-in-Chief, and your focus is on your client only, and all they want to do is bitch about their spouses. The expression TMI quickly comes into play here as they share tidbits about their extramarital affairs, and like a therapist, you know deep down they wonder what it would be like to hop into the sack with you. The personal trainer's personality is critical to making the morning routine as entertaining as possible because most clients dread the working out part of working out. Soon, the workout becomes secondary, the incessant chit-chatting primary, and before long, you're servicing the client's emotional well-being, negating the reason you are there in the first place. What becomes paramount is the intimate relationship that you establish with your client to get them addicted to you and the endorphins, in that order. Being in control determines the longevity of the relationship. Rarely does it end happily ever after. But you do find yourself saying, "You look great!" a lot.

My favorite clients were a married couple who owned a lovely home on The Strand in Manhattan Beach. Five days a week, I was hired to walk each of them up and down the boardwalk while listening intently to their life stories. Arriving at sunrise, I was usually finished by 8:00 AM. It was a cushy gig because they were both such lovely people.

Alas, there was a downside to all of this bopping around rich people's homes. The dreaded process of stretching out the clients was the worst part of being a trainer. Most often, clients haven't showered since the prior morning and have slept and snored in a pool of sweat. By the time you arrive bright-eyed and bushy-tailed to drag their sorry asses out of bed, they have day-old body odor so that once you finish their "workout," the stench leaves much to be desired. And clients love being stretched out. What felt good to them was way too much body contact for me. Trainers must develop an abnormal ability to hold their breath for long periods AND talk at the same time. This talent may later in life be accessed to seek a new career as a deep-sea diving instructor or Donald Trump's assistant.

This daily routine left many hours in which to kill time. It also provided an opportunity to attend the AA meetings that Lee had told me about. The meetings were held above a pizza parlor on Santa Monica Blvd. The WeHo Clubhouse had daily noon meetings filled with unemployed actors, models, porn stars, and hookers. Many of the attendees were gay men. There were several apparent lesbians and one beautiful, bosomy, straight Grace Kelly type who seemed out of place. I sidled up to her, and we became fast friends and workout partners. She also had a few "personal training" clients.

Remember when cable access channels were popular? Local cable stations needed to fill countless hours of blank airtime and offered to rent their makeshift studios for twenty-five dollars an hour, complete with a camera and cameraperson. Countless hours of nonsensical programming were being aired. When I lived in New York, Wendy Williams had a popular show covering red-carpet events, and look what that did for her. Megan and I started developing a reality fitness show called *Abe-N-Babe*, which was quite promising. The show's premise: Abe-N-Babe would go from gym to gym and from juice bar to juice bar, interviewing fitness addicts. Everyone at Gold's wanted to be a guest on the show. Sadly, Megan found the man of her dreams, got married, and moved to Arizona, thwarting the inevitable success of the *Abe-N-Babe* show. Between the annoyance of dealing with sweaty middle-aged humans and Megan leaving me, my fitness guru career seemed fleeting and that it wasn't going to be my life's work. Something had to give.

OY

Abandoned by my blonde bombshell, I was welcomed into a group of lovely, funny queens dealing with similar issues in Gay AA. We became a tight-knit group of recovering addicts who, for the most part, were hilarious, bitchy queens, mostly drug addicts. The meetings were social, especially on Saturday nights and Sunday brunches. Being new to LA, I found it a comforting environment. In addition to being sequestered within the fellowship that comes with the program, somehow, I met a person that people in AA would call a "normy"—someone who did not have a drinking or drug problem and could have one glass of wine and call it a day. Lindsay was my "normy." We had a sweet romance that led to my moving in with him after only a few months of dating. My comrades in AA couldn't believe I had found someone so quickly and warned me not to get involved in a relationship during my first year of sobriety. But, hey, hate the play, not the player.

Everyone in AA, being hyper-conscientious, was getting tested for AIDS, as the gay community was on tenterhooks because countless people were still dying every day from the dreaded disease. Yes, there was the discovery of AZT, which was purported to be a miracle drug for the virus, but it turned out not to be great for gay men. Instead, it was more effective in preventing mothers from passing it on to their babies.

After a midday AA meeting, our crew spontaneously decided to get tested at the West Hollywood clinic. We trotted off, giggling and carrying on without a care in the world, unconcerned that any of us would test positive. I didn't even tell Lindsay I was going for the test because it was like any other innocent AA group outing, like going to the mall or lunch at the Urth Cafe. We arrived at the clinic, a cold, hectic atmosphere with many young men and several black women waiting for blood tests. The vibe in the room was tense. Our carefree act ceased immediately. We huddled in the back of the room after signing our names to the list. The wait to get our blood tests was not as bad as we had imagined. We thought we would get results then and there; we would all be negative and then frolic off on our merry way. We were told that they would contact us individually within a week and that we had to return to the clinic for results. The policy was that no results were given over the phone, regardless of the test outcome, and our merry afternoon turned into a total buzz kill. We decided not to tell anyone that we had been tested. Suddenly, I felt like I had a red A tattooed on my forehead.

For a whole week, I pushed the fact that I was waiting for a call from the clinic to the back of my mind. That's one of the benefits of denial. We can push things so far down from having to think about them that it's like everything is "fine," especially when it's not. It can be a gift or an albatross, depending on the outcome of what you are in denial of. A classic AA slogan: "Denial is not a river in Egypt."

Exactly one week after I was tested, I got a call to come in for my results.

"There is no way I am positive," I kept telling myself. I was positive that I *wasn't* positive. Positively *not* positive.

Dear God,

Please disregard all prior requests. Nothing is as important as what I'm about to ask—correction, beg—you for. Please, God, let me be negative. You fucking better not do that to me after everything we've been through.

Love,

ABE

P.S. I mean, I'd rather be fat.

The ride over to the nerve-wracking, sterile clinic was depressing. I was told to wait in a small room with nothing besides a metal desk and two metal folding chairs. It was so sterile—not a piece of paper or a poster on the gray walls, nothing. I waited for what felt like an eternity. Suddenly, it occurred to me that I was about to get terrible news. My blood ran cold, my hands were sweaty, and I wanted to leave the room and run away. As I got up to leave, the door swung open and a heavy-set, bearded guy, a gay bear wearing khaki pants and a blue T-shirt, holding a manila folder, rushed in, not looking at me, just down at the folder, and told me to sit down.

"I'm sorry to tell you, but your results show that you are HIV-positive and your T-cell count is very low. We suggest you start taking AZT at once." He handed me a big blue-and-white bottle and said, "Take 12 pills a day. Four at breakfast, four at lunch, and four at dinner."

"What?" Tears started welling up. "That can't be. Are you sure?"

"Yes. I'm sorry," he said, still looking at the paperwork and not at me, making no attempt to comfort someone who had just been given a death sentence. He must have gotten too used to delivering bad news.

"Can I take the test again? Maybe it's a mistake?" I was desperate and getting hysterical.

"I don't know what to tell you, man." He closed the folder and started toward the door. "I have to go."

Devoid of bedside manners, the Bad News Bear made his abrupt exit. I had been left alone in a dank room that would remain in my mind till the day I died, which I hoped and prayed would not be soon.

I was afraid to call Lindsay, who worked at KCAL News. Lindsay was the total opposite of me, a strait-laced, serious, hard-working, tax-paying, generous-to-a-fault, buttoned-up soul. When we had first met at a bar, I noticed he was drinking a bottle of water. I had never seen him at a meeting. He was tall, sandy blond, handsome, and fit, with the thickest lips I had ever seen. Keep in mind this was way before people started injecting fillers. He noticed me noticing him, and that started our connection. He was darling; we talked till dawn, and I was smitten. He asked me to move in after a few months, like lesbians who U-Haul their way through relationships. I had lived with Lindsay for a few months when this horrendous situation presented itself. It's not as though he could have left the studio to come get me because he was working on a live broadcast. Besides, I was freaking out and afraid to tell him the bad news, not knowing how he would react. AIDS was still a death sentence, and loved ones had legitimate concerns about how it would impact their lives.

The better call to make was to my friend, LeeAnne, an executive at Universal Studios. When I decided to move to LA, she had generously offered me her extra bedroom for those first few weeks while I was getting situated. LeeAnne and I had lived in the same apartment building in Gramercy Park in NYC in the mid-1980s. It was like a college dorm, with many young people living in lofts, partying nightly. We rarely left the building during the winters since drug dealers, delis, and diners delivered. We were all freelancers and never knew what anyone did for money, but somehow, there was always enough cash among us to sustain us for another evening of languishing in white powder and vodka. Life in Gramercy Park was so much—too much—fun. The "good life" was so *not* great that it launched my investigation into Alcoholics Anonymous. LeeAnne was the only one in the building with a real job, and she was the first to get out of our psycho Dodge City and move to LA.

I called LeeAnne's office from a pay phone and spoke to her assistant, trying not to bawl uncontrollably.

"LeeAnne is in a meeting, can I get a number for a return?" (That's entertainment industry lingo.)

I sobbed and blurted, "Please tell her it's an emergency." She put me on hold, and LeeAnne was on the phone within seconds. When I heard her voice, I completely went to pieces and couldn't talk. I didn't want to hear myself say those awful words out loud: "I just tested positive for HIV." Maybe if I didn't say it, it wouldn't be true. Maybe I was dreaming or nightmaring. What was going to happen now? Was my life over? I was only thirty-three years old! I was just friggin' getting started. I hadn't written a word yet!

"What happened? Where are you?"

I was crying and couldn't get any words out.

"Abe, tell me." LeeAnne sounded concerned; I could hear her voice beginning to crack.

"LeeAnne, I'm, I'm, I'm… damn it. What am I gonna do? Oh my God. This is it."

"What is it, what? Tell me. Are you okay? Did you have an accident?"

"I just tested positive".

LeeAnne shrieked, "What? Where are you?"

"What am I gonna do?"

"Where are you? I'm coming to get you. I'll be there as soon as I can."

"Oh LeeAnne…" Choking back the tears, I told her where I was: HELL.

I waited, weeping, until I saw LeeAnne pull up in her uncle's vintage, sky-blue convertible Cutlass Supreme with the top down.

"Hop in here, you."

I complied and broke down in her arms. She held me tightly and we cried. We had come a long way from Gramercy Park. In our many nights of joy back east, we had shared no tragedies, considering how many overdoses never happened. This was the test of a friendship that has lasted to this day. LeeAnne took me on a long ride to Malibu to watch the sunset. We sat in silence as I cried. She turned to me, grabbed my shoulders, and said, "We will get through this. YOU are going to get through this. Do you hear me?"

I wanted to believe her, but I'd resigned myself to dying young like my dad, whose dad had also died young. But *this* young? This had to be a mistake. I'd have to take this up with God.

During one lifetime, how many times can you say, "Today will live in infamy"? In the same way that the Greatest Generation remembers Pearl Harbor, we, too, experience critical historical or personal moments that change the trajectory of our lives forever. Case in point: the Kennedy Assassination. Everyone remembers where they were when they heard that JFK was murdered in Dallas. It's the same with 9/11, the moment you saw the first plane hit the World Trade Center. We all clock deeply personal events and experiences that traumatize us, be it a parent dying unexpectedly or a near-death situation. These moments force us to dig deeper internally to process loss, pain, and suffering. I have had more than my fair share of these catastrophes, but none as catastrophically horrendous as the day I tested positive.

A heart attack at fifty was beginning to sound like a dream scenario, which was my father's age when he died—speaking of a day of infamy. Then I thought about my mother, the amazingly strong woman who had survived the horrors of the Holocaust. Would I survive this? Could

I find the will to battle this chromosomal Nazi? Would this be my war to fight within myself? We talked about the meaning of life and what really mattered now. I was still so afraid to tell Lindsay, but LeeAnne assured me that he loved me and would be very understanding.

We drove back to West Hollywood, and en route to dropping me off, she pulled me into The Pleasure Chest, an adult entertainment store on Santa Monica Boulevard.

"What are we doing here?" I asked.

"I'm buying you a dildo, honey. You are going to need one." And somehow, we laughed and, together, arm in arm, giggled our way through the aisles of sex toys. Perhaps she was right that I would get through this. We would get through this together.

LeeAnne stayed with me until Lindsay came home after his shift on the *Ten O'Clock News*. It was awkward, but he was understanding and comforting. He immediately got tested. Thank God he was negative, and we refrained from that kind of physical contact, which ultimately changed our relationship to that of friends more than anything else. Sure, I had a crushing feeling of being damaged goods, but more than that, I understood the fear.

Speaking of which, I had to tell my family the riveting news. I was disappointed that my sisters didn't jump on a plane to hold my hand, which back then was not something people wanted to do. I loved them anyway, but they were no Princess Diana. So I get it. We decided that my mother's knowing was not required because HIV was a complicated issue, especially with the media reporting it as a death sentence. We didn't want her thrown into a quagmire of sadness and understandable fear. Thankfully, my new adoptive family in LA got me through the worst of it.

Turns out, I was the only one in my AA group who had tested positive that day. When I shared the news with them, they were incredible and helped me through the tragic time during which I had to accept the challenge that had presented itself. It was an opportunity to test my spiritual resolve to live one day at a time and let the inner demons be damned. Determined to survive, I started downing three gallons of water a day, convinced I would flush this shit out of my system, not to mention the havoc that the toxins of AZT were wreaking. There's no telling why I am still alive while so many aren't, but more than anything, my belief system, coupled with my survivor DNA, is part and parcel of why I am still here to tell my story.

> *Dear God,*
> *Thank you for giving me some good material to help me get*
> *started on my great American novel. Would it be asking too*
> *much for you to keep me alive until that shit's done?*
> *Love,*
> *ABE*

THERE'S NO BUSINESS LIKE SHOW BUSINESS

"Never work with children or animals."
–Old Hollywood Adage–W.C. Fields

"Nobody knows anything."
–Old Hollywood Adage–William Goldman

nce you've lived in LA for more than a year, you're considered an unofficial official resident. With that honor comes an obligation to try your hand at screenwriting. Everyone who is anyone has a screenplay they are working on or have "just finished." Others are racking their brains, fleshing out storylines in their heads, while the rest of us are in writing workshops. One cannot properly exist in La La Land without being able to say, "I am writing a screenplay." If Descartes lived here, he would have said, "I am writing a screenplay. Therefore, I am." It's practically illegal not to at least say that you and a friend are "collaborating on a project." Naturally, you are better off telling anyone who will listen that you are "in development" on a project and not at liberty to discuss it. "I signed an NDA; you know how that is."

My neighbor Joanne was a "screenwriter" who actually had a script optioned, which is a heroic accomplishment in that she made at least one dollar for all the hard work it took not only to labor through finishing a feature-length script but also to schmooze around town until she got a producer to give it a shot. Another Hollywood adage is, "A producer is someone who knows a writer." Sadly, the film went into turnaround and never got made.

Speaking of Hollywood adages, it has been said that if you take a great script and toss it out of your car window on the 405, it will still end up getting made. Joanne loved telling the story about a studio head who threatened her lackeys (I mean, executives) after a dismal weekend box office: "Get the hell out of my office and don't come back till you find a script that can make us some fucking money. I don't care if you go scour the fucking 405 Freeway; anything is better than the shit you idiots are green lighting."

Joanne insisted I take Robert McKee's Story Seminar, considered "the only" screenwriting workshop in Hollywood. Everyone who was anyone in the business had taken his class. Ask me if McKee has received an Oscar ®, an Emmy ®, or a Golden Globe ®. I couldn't stop wondering if Woody Allen's adage about "canning and doing" applied here.

The classes were interesting, and McKee encouraged us to rewatch movies with a different perspective and to try our hand at writing scenes. As with acting, a good rule of thumb for writing good dialogue is to be a good listener. As someone who took pride in eavesdropping, I spent an afternoon at Erewhon Market before taking my first crack at dialogue starring pretentious people.

INT. -   EREWHON – MIDDAY (Strewn with unemployed actors
          and screenwriters)

GIRL: (Frustrated) I AM happy.

BOY: Really?

GIRL: Yes, really. Why are you asking?

BOY: Are you sure?

GIRL: Is there a problem?

BOY: I'm feeling a bit distant lately.

GIRL: Well, not sure why that is.

BOY: Since I haven't been getting too much work lately and can't
         get you nice things.

GIRL: Things don't make me happy.

BOY: What makes you happy?

GIRL: You really wanna know what makes me happy? Spin classes
         make me happy. Writing my screenplay with Devin makes
         me happy. Are you happy now?

END SCENE

Script Note (official lingo): So much was said yet unsaid in that cryptic conversation as GIRL and BOY spoke in circles, where clearly there is no love lost. Read between the lines; you can see that GIRL admits without actually saying that she is fucking DEVIN during their screenwriting sessions. This conversation is the prelude to their impending break-up. Was GIRL even writing a script with DEVIN, or was that a ruse to get out of the house? GIRL was sick of BOY, a grossly underemployed actor with a drinking habit. By the time those two leave Erewhon, silence will fall between them, like in a scene from a Terrence Malick film. Begging the question, does Terrence Malick shop at Erewhon?

Writing is hard, and not for everyone. Daily journaling is a painful experience for most, no matter what Oprah says. If I ever was to become a writer, perhaps I could find a job with a real screenwriter, get on-the-job training, and be a fly on the wall in a room where the magic of Hollywood happens. Would that be too much to hope for? I'd even be willing to be a lackey and get Starbucks for the right lackey's lackey of a kick-ass writer. For now, I'd be willing to be a lackey's lackey, but it would have to be for someone groovy. I couldn't be just anybody's lackey.

THE CHORE WHORE

As luck would have it, I bumped into a grade school friend, Alan, at Jones on Third one afternoon while the line crawled at a snail's pace. We had enough time to recap the fifteen years that had passed since our last encounter at a gay bar in NYC. Feigning interest in his addiction journey, I then shared my harrowing tale of woe and career disappointments, embellishing where possible to make my saga sound more dire. Truth is, recovering addicts exaggerate, thirsty for accolades for simply and finally taking care of ourselves. No applause necessary.

Alan was working in the business as a "Chore Whore" to a well-known has-been. "Chore Whore" is one of the more loving names assigned to celebrity assistants.

> SIDEBAR: In Hollywood, either you ARE talent, or you're sucking up to talent—rarely the twain shall meet. Alas, that's how the star-making hierarchy goes in this constellation of mattering. And the sooner you accept that fact, the farther you will go.

Alan was moving back East to join his family's real estate business since he had just about had enough of all the Hollywood bullshit. He had enjoyed much of the hayride working for Mr. Self-Absorbed, but he'd finally had quite enough. Alan wanted to do something that didn't keep him awake at night worrying about unbridled minutiae that had nothing to do with his life. He needed to nurture his own spiritual, mental, and physical health. Chore Whores have to put their own best interests to one side—the back, usually. Alan was tasked with finding his own replacement since that's not the kind of job one posts on public forums where lunatics and sycophants abound.

"Would you be interested?" Alan asked me.

The timing of the job offer seemed fortuitous.

"That would be amazing."

How hard could being a celebrity assistant be? I envisioned myself running errands, chatting with other celebrities, shopping, thumbing through magazines, and updating my boss on what was on Page Six.

Mr. Self-Absorbed wasn't someone I admired much, not having heard hide-nor-hair from him for years since he had slipped into obscurity. There was tabloid talk of drug addiction, overdose, bisexuality, divorce, and all the typical Hollywood fodder, coupled with having a string of flops. The following week I went to his walled-off compound in Mandeville Canyon, home to many elusive, and illusive, celebrity has-beens.

Mandeville Canyon was a bit of a commute from West Hollywood, and this guy had better be worth the schlep before I'd sign on for this routine twice a day. When I arrived at the house, Alan answered the door and whispered, "He's not in a great mood."

"What should I do?"

"Wait in the den, and I'll be right back."

Alan walked me to a cavernous library filled with books and countless pictures of this celebrity from back in the day. There was a massive painting of him over the fireplace. Love yourself much? I already dreaded meeting him after waiting for half an hour before Alan returned to say, "Oy."

"What's the matter?" I asked, annoyed.

"He just got back from the doctor's office and…"

"Oh, no, is it bad news?" I asked.

"Only if you could see his face. He's been 'seeing' this cosmetic surgeon and had some kind of lift or something yesterday, and yikes."

That's the thing about Hollywood has-beens. They dread aging more than most humans and will stop at nothing to reverse or halt the process. Scarfing pills and booze, they preserve their psycho-psyches in denial of who they *aren't* anymore. The fillers and Botox keep their faces from falling, but they don't know when to leave well enough alone. As if they were marinating a slab of pork, they pickle their faces and slather on anything that promises youth-enhancing results. Knowing they are not important enough to get a star on the Walk of Fame, celebrities like Mr. Self-Absorbed will only be remembered at the crossroads of Hollywood and Brine.

Alan said apologetically, "We have to reschedule."

"Actually, no, we don't." I thanked him. For what, I didn't know, besides learning that I had no intention of schlepping to the nether regions of Sunset Boulevard on a daily basis to deal with a self-absorbed, aging lunatic. In fact, I thanked Alan for teaching me what I would NOT do to stay in Hollywood, which was being treated disrespectfully by a disrespectful oaf.

When I arrived home, I got a call from Jessie. Yes, *that* Jessie, whom I hadn't seen in eons, who had also moved to LA a few years ago. She heard that I moved to L.A., called, suggested meeting for lunch, and I was happy to do so. We met at Mauro Cafe at Fred Segal Melrose, where I told her about my silly job interview and mentioned that I needed a new client or two. Jessie had created an interesting gig for herself as chore whoring goes. She was more like an uber-lackey in that she managed several celebrity clients and handled all their day-to-day needs and schedules from her home-based command center. Jessie farmed out the chore-whoring grunt work to her lackey's lackeys, who did the grocery and toiletry shopping, picking up dry cleaning—you know, the shitty part.

Jessie was working with arguably the coolest woman in Hollywood, Lily Hunter, a prolific writer, actress, and daughter of a screen legend. Lily had just given birth to her first child and needed additional hands-on support that was very specific. I adored Lily Hunter; she was one of my heroes. Jessie mentioned that Lily needed someone to help get her motivated to do what she did best: write, and that she was behind on a couple of projects.

In addition to earning a reputation as a gifted writer, Lily had become a rare, sought-after commodity known in Hollywood as a script doctor. She would be called into the studio to fix a script. Each project had different needs, either punching up the dialogue, reworking whole scenes, or sometimes doing page one rewrites—anything to improve the flat dialogue that had already been greenlit and, in some cases, had started filming, which proved lackluster.

■

SCRIPT SCRUB NURSE

t's been said that you should never meet your heroes, yet off I went, winding up another Beverly hill, climbing to an altitude where my ears popped like I was on a descending airplane. I arrived at a small metal box standing in front of a roadblock designed to keep the riff raff at a distance from the royal ilk living inside Alice's Looking Glass. That's one way to protect the "talent" from the rabid fans, stalkers, and autograph hounds while the gatekeepers—publicists, agents, and managers—shield their A-list clients from unwanted "others" like the tabloid media and assorted lunatics.

"I'm here to see Lily Hunter," I said sheepishly after pressing the button and hearing some static.

"Name dropper," the instantly recognizable voice garbled sarcastically from the call box—the first indication that I was going to love this woman.

The barricades miraculously lowered into the ground, and so began my foray into the madcap world of La La Land. Having made it through the looking glass, I took a private, narrow road to a cozy ski-lodge-looking house on a hill.

I pulled up to yet another small metal box at the foot of a driveway blocked by a wooden walled gate featuring an animated mural and thought to myself, "Well, Dorothy, we're not in New Jersey anymore." Again, I buzzed a similar box, and the gate slowly swung open. I was delighted to see this wonderland full of quirky objects like a gigantic fiberglass camel peeking its head out from a bush, chandeliers hanging from trees, water fountains, and ridiculous statues. Everywhere I looked, something else revealed more and more of Lily's personality.

A zaftig Black woman, Betty, popped her head out from the kitchen door and waved me in. The warm, vintage 1940s-style kitchen, complete with gingham curtains, cherry-print seat cushions, and collectible tchotchkes everywhere, was enhanced by an aroma of deliciousness. A talk show blared on the small TV beside the range where chicken was frying, collard greens were boiling, and corn muffins were cooling.

"This place smells like heaven," I smiled.

"Well, if you want a corn muffin and some coffee, sit yourself down; Lily's finishing up a call," Betty ordered in an inviting way.

"Oh, you don't need to bother," I said, not wanting to make myself a chore but unable to resist.

I could hear Lily outside by the pool chatting on the phone. I swigged the rest of the coffee to get the cakey corn muffin crumbs off my teeth and was ushered out to the swimming pool… movie star. I felt like a hillbilly in Beverly Hills. Birds were chirping, the calming sound of a water fountain serenaded us. This place was more of a Wonderland than Oz. A scruffy, black nerf-herder of a dog, BooBoo, came bouncing over to me. I sat awkwardly at the edge of a lounge chair and watched Lily chatting on the phone. She was listening more than talking, and she glanced at me and waved. Petting BooBoo while being careful not to tip the chair forward was a Wallenda-like task. Lily lit a Marlboro Light and tried cutting off whoever was monopolizing the conversation. She winked and said,

"I'll call you back. I think I just heard the baby." She hung up the phone, turned, took a drag of the smoke, and commented, "People love sharing their parenting skills."

"Hi," I muttered.

"The best way to get off a call with someone who loves talking about themselves is saying you just heard the baby."

"Duly noted."

"Hi, Abe. That's not a name you hear a lot."

"Yeah, especially out here."

"Jewish?"

"Is it the nose or my name? What gave it away?"

"Both. I'm half Jewish. Which makes me Jew–ish."

SIDEBAR: Although lowlife George Santos tried and failed to usurp the expression "Jew–ish," proving what a piece of shit he is, I will always attribute that line to Lily Hunter.

Lily took another drag on her cigarette, put it out, and said, "How do you know Jessie?"

"We went to middle school together and almost got arrested on the day of the Moratorium to End the War in Vietnam."

"Jessie?"

"And we were Studio 54 club kids."

"I can see that."

"I'm a refugee from the fashion industry. Speaking of refugees, my parents were Holocaust survivors." Shit, I thought, I'm rambling.

"Holocaust, huh? My parents survived Louis B. Mayer."

"No place is safe."

Grinning, she asked, "Do you like children?"

"Love kids."

"Good. My baby girl Olivia is the primary purpose around here," she said proudly.

"Well, I have six nieces and nephews. I'm like Super Uncle, not Uncle Vanya."

"Let's see if you Cry Uncle. Follow me."

"Definitely not Uncle Sam."

This easy repartee would continue into the next century, punctuating our complicated, joyous relationship. We walked into the charming, bohemian-chic home, past endless collectible art and tchotchkes. One painting of a monkey in a pink dress with a floral head covering was most engaging and a sign of things to come. We passed an enormous, framed outtake of the Cowardly Lion Makeup Test en route to the baby's room. Olivia was sound asleep; Lily motioned me to follow her into the living room, where we sat and drank Coca-Colas and continued chatting.

"When she wakes up, I'd like to see how she reacts when you try to pick her up."

"I'm telling you, babies, parents, and dogs love me."

Being the same age as well as recovering addicts kept our conversation lively as we discovered all the things we had in common. We discussed our love of old movies, gossip, sobriety, and dogs. The nanny brought Olivia to Lily and kissed her head. We agreed that the smell of babies' heads was intoxicating and remarked on the fact that it was the only libation allowed us these days.

Olivia started fussing in her mother's arms. I reached out, Lily handed her over, and she settled onto my chest. We continued talking while the reverberations of my lower-baritone voice soothed her, and she quieted immediately. Within seconds, Olivia's eyes closed.

"When can you start?"

Lily pushed the intercom on the phone sitting beside her and called for Betty, who appeared in seconds.

"What do you think, Bet? Should we hire him?"

Nothing in daily life prepares you for working for a celebrity, especially one like Lily. She was incredibly smart, funny, and inquisitive.

"I don't know, Lily," Betty chimed in sarcastically, nodding her head yes.

"Like you could live without me? How's tomorrow?"

I got up, handed Olivia to the nanny, attempted to hug Betty, and left. And so began the roller coaster ride, and life would never be the same.

Careening down Benedict Canyon after the interview with Lily, I thought, "That was a piece of cake." If you were to ask me at any point before that day what I'd be doing with my life, which included having your druthers, never in a million years would "working for Lily Hunter in the intimacy of her boudoir, being privy to the creation of some of her best work" be my answer. This gig was a dream opportunity to learn firsthand the nuances of writing. Having a front-row seat to the daunting process of writing a novel was beyond a novel opportunity, something to be relished. Who doesn't believe deep down in their heart that they have a book in them? As they say, "Those who can, do. Those who can't…." Seriously, can you picture me being a gym teacher?

Sigmund Freud said, "We are here to love and work," which, up until then, was my gray area. I couldn't decide if I needed to love work or be willing to work towards love, although love took way too much work. Now you can see why I was in therapy. At least working for Lily presented an opportunity to love work.

The next day, when I arrived at work, Lily said she had some bad news for me. My heart sank. I immediately thought Lily had somehow found out that I was HIV-positive and Olivia's pediatrician had insisted that I be let go. Although two years had passed since

I tested positive, it was always at the forefront of my mind. Doctors back then still had concerns about HIV-positive people interacting with children.

"You have to go meet my mother in the Valley," she said.

Phew, what a relief. But how could meeting Aurora Haynes be bad news?

"Why is that bad news?" I asked.

"You'll see. I love my mother; you will, too. She'll insist on giving you the third degree. She does that to everyone. You'll be fine." Famous last words; for all I knew, I was off to meet the Queen of Hearts, who could easily put a kibosh on this dream gig.

With aplomb and a pit in my stomach, having no idea what to expect, I headed over to Aurora Haynes' home. Did I just say that? En route, I called my sisters to tell them what my chore of the day was. Rita said, "I want details."

Following Lily's directions to the Valley, I expected a far more glamorous neighborhood and more than a modest, split-level ranch house on a nondescript street in North Hollywood. Rita would be disappointed. I sheepishly rang the melodic chimes and a white-haired, middle-aged man appeared, speaking ever so softly, and welcomed me into the overly decorated, dark home that was eerily quiet.

Countless black-and-white signed pictures of iconic celebrities with Aurora were on display throughout the hallway as I was led to the living room of one of the few remaining true Hollywood legends.

"Would you like a beverage?" Chester asked. He reminded me of the Ghost of Christmas Past, wisping through the house slowly and silently as if floating on air. Perhaps it was the overly plush carpeting coupled with his velvet slippers that made him appear to hover ever so slightly. I waited patiently for Aurora Haynes to appear. When she did, she was dressed like Norma Desmond in *Sunset Boulevard*: turban, silk robe, velvet slippers.

"Hello, dear, I'm Aurora Haynes."

"Of course, the one and only."

"And you're Abe? My second husband's business manager was an Abe. We found out later, rather too late, to what extent Abe was managing his affairs by gambling away all our money."

What does one say to that introduction? "Ummmm." I was at a loss for words, which is rare, as anyone who knows me would attest. "Well, for starters, I'm not that kind of Abe," I said quickly.

"So tell me, what kind of Abe are you?" Lily's imitation of how her mother spoke had been spot on. Aurora had graduated from the MGM School of Diction during the Golden Age of Hollywood.

Chester whooshed in, carrying a tray with a bottle of Riesling, a large goblet, a can of Coca-Cola, and a tall ice-tumbler.

"Thanks, nothing for me," I said once again, not wanting to be a bother.

"These are Miss Aurora's. Are you sure I can't get you something to drink?"

"There's nothing like a tall glass of Coca-Cola with plenty of ice," Aurora said, smiling as Chester poured the beverages for her. "Have one with me."

That warm invitation was a great icebreaker, and soon enough, we were toasting to good health and Lily and the baby. I drank, still hoping my HIV-positive status was not going to come up in conversation. Aurora talked me through her better days, failed marriages, and why she no longer had eyebrows. It was riveting, although minutes crept by like hours, and I felt like I had fallen through the Rabbit Hole. She finally asked, "What are your intentions with Lily?"

"Intentions? I intend to help her in any way I can. She's fantastic."

"She sure is. But you have to be very patient with her. She is very sensitive." Tears began to well up. "She's had a difficult life, you know."

Difficult? "Charmed" was more along the lines of the life she must have led compared to my Weehawken excuse for a childhood. But okay, each of us has a cross to bear. I assured Aurora that my intentions were more than honorable and that I wanted to be an integral part of Lily's support team and, more specifically, keep her writing. She shed a few more tears when she spoke of how much she loved her daughter.

Awkward as it was, I adored this eccentric anomaly with achingly youthful skin. I almost asked for her beauty regimen but stopped myself. My mother had taught me to slather on the Helena Rubinstein at a young age. For years, it became hard to find in the U.S., so I've tried everything and anything since then.

What had started out as fun was now getting exhausting, being twirled up into Aurora's aura. I couldn't reassure her enough that I would take good care of her precious Lily as if she were my very own sister. I was beginning to feel a bit claustrophobic from all the smotherly love. I tactfully excused myself, stepping backward to escape this peculiar Dodge. "We have an early start tomorrow." There was no air kiss goodbye, just her hand extended to me as if I should kiss the ring.

Chester escorted me to the door and gave me a look that said more than a thousand words, almost like a warning to "Beware" combined with a plea for help. He was a kind soul. But I couldn't get myself back to the other side of the Valley—the right side—fast enough.

That night, I got a call from Jessie telling me that I had to tell Lily about my HIV-positive status because of the baby. Her straight husband insisted. That was truly terrifying, as it could end this incredibly unreal opportunity, so I begged Jessie to let me be the one to tell her. Even though Lily was arguably the coolest woman in Hollywood,

I was still at the mercy of other people's fears and ignorance. In 1992, there were still plenty of both. My new life flashed before my eyes. There was a possibility that this major moment could be taken away for a reason that was totally out of my control. It destroyed my confidence. For eighteen hours, I was in a state of panic and dread. I couldn't bear having the impending confrontation. I prepared mentally for a showdown, and before I went to work, I mustered the courage to call Lily before heading back up the long, winding road.

Her response to my disclosure was "Just don't you dare try having sex with Olivia. Otherwise, get up here; we got shit to do."

The next day, when I arrived, Lily hugged me. I started to cry, and we just held each other for a meaningful moment. She told me a personal story about one of her good friends who died of AIDS, whom she had taken into her home to care for until his death. That level of compassion was beyond admirable. In fact, it was very Princess Di of her. The kindness and respect Lily showed at my most vulnerable moment helped me through a personal battle of not feeling like a leper. I will forever owe Lily a debt of gratitude for the grace she showed me.

Lily transcended traditional Hollywood trash due to her royal pedigree. She brought together the most diverse and interesting groups of people and hosted countless dinner parties with artists, architects, writers, actors, directors, musicians, and drug addicts, recovering or otherwise. Falling into the latter category, I appreciated her collection of collagenous junkies and the fact that it didn't matter who you were and what you did to get invited to the table. I began to feel a sense of belonging. It didn't take long to feel as though these people were no better than me just because of their position in the hierarchy of Hollywood. I'd come full circle from the days when I was awestruck by the movie stars on the silver screen.

Days later, the most orgasmic tidbit of gossip dropped on the house like an atom bomb. The story goes like this: Lily got a phone call, interrupted our writing jag, and instantly began gasping for air as she listened intently to what she was being told.

"What?" she asked in a tone of disbelief and horror. "What? What?" she repeated, gasping to a crescendo of gaspiness. "Are you fucking kidding?"

Desperate to hear what was being said, I hoped it wasn't bad news because this gasping situation sounded much more severe than the usual gossip that included who was sleeping with whom in Hollywood. I tried to act nonchalant, since it was still early days of my gig and I had to act cool.

"How did she find out? (Pause, gasp.) That's terrible."

I could no longer contain myself and motioned to Lily that I needed to know what was happening.

I mouthed, "What, what, what???"

Lily said, "You mean I can't tell anyone this? I promise I won't, but can you do me a favor and just say it again, one more time, so I can hear it because it is just so unbelievable?"

Lily winked at me, smiling, and pushed the speaker button on the phone so the person would be audible to me while blurting out the most gigantic kernel of dish in Hollywood history. Lily kept her promise, and I got to get the dish. The generosity of that gesture made me fall more in love with her—madly, truly, deeply.

Someone from Woody Allen's camp had confided in Lily about his affair with Mia Farrow's adopted daughter, Soon Yi. Lily was told this before it became public knowledge, and she was sworn to secrecy.

This Woody Allen incident gloriously vindicated me from the day I warned that I would crush him for what he'd done to us unsuspecting New Jerseyites. Knowing that he was more than squirming at that very moment was all the just desserts I had craved since childhood.

THE END OF THE AFFAIR

My relationship with Peter was never going to survive Hollywood. That much was clear. We were polar opposites, and one of us was leaning toward being bipolar; hence, the handwriting was on the wall. If the word *respect* loses its applicability, or unless you're a glutton for punishment, there's little hope in "living happily ever after." Too many Hollywood fairytale romances have ended poorly. Liz and Dick, Lucy and Ricky, Sonny and Cher. Not that I'm comparing Peter and me to Liz and Dick, but all romances that come to an end feel like a bad Hollywood ending. Naturally, we all yearn for that cinematic, sweeping, long shot where we see ourselves as that happy couple walking off into the sunset. Dramatic music swells, implying "and they lived happily ever after." Fade to black.

Life's not like that. Surely, mine and Peter's wasn't at the end. We were about to celebrate (for lack of a better word) our seventh anniversary. So, you can only imagine how long it had been since we'd had good sex. Admit it: after a few years in most romantic relationships, straight or gay, romance and sex take a different turn, and not necessarily ON. We settled into a brotherly kind of roommate-slash-friendship sans benefits situation that was so far removed from where it started. We were finally nearing the end of our endless affair. What began as "I will love you till the day I die" was now more like, "Let's end this fairy tale, and do fairy tale endings exist?"

SIDEBAR: Being gay didn't automatically classify our relationship as a "fairy" tale. Frankly, it had become more of a Brothers Grimm situation; you know, it starts off sugary sweet, then quickly turns into a scary life lesson. Don't talk to wolves à la *Little Red Riding Hood*, avoid witches who cook à la *Hansel & Gretel*, and be your own Prince Charming à la *Cinderella*.

It's too bad that by 2001, when all this was going on, the Internet hadn't exploded. Perhaps we could have Googled "healthy relationships" and stumbled upon the website, And They Lived Happily Ever After dot com, and taken the love quiz "How to Save Your Marriage." We could have pawed through articles like "The Three Big Mistakes in Every Relationship," "The Secret to Great Sex," or "Can You Ever Really Know Someone?" Who knows if our relationship could have been salvaged? Despite the lovely LA weather, a cold winter chill settled between us, and "compromise" became a recurring buzzword in our daily dialogue. Besides, once the discussion turns to "Let's go to couple's counseling," you know there's trouble in paradise, and irreconcilable differences lurk on the horizon. Mmmm-hmmm. By that point, all roads were leading Peter back to Amsterdam, from whence he hailed, while I would remain in Los Angeles and maintain the last vestiges of chore whoring.

The fateful day came; I watched as he struggled to close the last suitcase. His favorite books had been taped up in a box—a box

I would naturally have to arrange to ship; destination: anywhere but here. Heavy sighs broke the silence, and all I could say was, "We should leave before the traffic gets unbearable." Though it wasn't what I wanted to say at all. The words I meant to string together were, "What the fuck are we doing? Are we going to regret this?" But they didn't fall trippingly off my tongue. The right words got stuck in my mouth, exploded like Pop Rocks, and dissolved. All I could do was act like I wanted to get to the airport on gossamer wings and not prolong the inevitable by getting stuck in LA rush hour traffic. God forbid he missed the flight. Nothing would be more depressing than that, coupled with a long, slow ride down the 10 and 101 Freeways in deathlike silence—both ways.

All I could think about now were the silly, lovable moments we had shared, like when we got locked out of the car in the pouring rain and couldn't stop laughing. Stranded in the middle of nowhere, I mustered up the courage to blurt out "I love you" to him for the first time, remembering how many times I had meant it. The feeling of oneness that I'd never experienced before and may never again. That was the risk here, for sure. Being the daddy breadwinner became uninteresting, and his need to be needy became unbearable, making this once beautiful boy somehow less attractive and less desirable.

"Here, do you need help with that?" I asked and got up to push down on the extra-large red-and-black plaid suitcase I knew would cost additional money for overweight baggage when he checked in for his flight. *I'd better hand him a couple hundred bucks before he gets out of the car,* I thought, not wanting to say it out loud as it might set him off. Our arms brushed against each other, and the reality of what was happening set in again, even deeper.

"Well, that does it," he grunted, struggling with the last few inches of the luggage's zipper. He stepped outside onto the huge patio and looked around at our most significant accomplishment, which sadly also represented the turning point when our relationship started going south. In an attempt to keep it together, we discovered our green thumbs and planted a wild orgy of exotic plants and shrubs: succulent night-blooming jasmine, rosemary bushes, and morning glories that climbed the veranda to our upstairs bedroom and woke us with their sweet fragrance. We made endless trips to Home Depot and the Sunset Boulevard Nursery. The guys there knew us well and must've thought we were happy homemakers. Only we weren't.

The silence was deafening as we loaded the car until Peter called for the dogs to join us. Dogs have an uncanny way of knowing when something is going horribly wrong. They look at you with big, sad eyes, heads tilted to one side. As soon as the luggage comes out, Woodstock knows something is afoot. He and Alfie jumped into the front seat and perched themselves on the dashboard like navigators-in-chief.

"Are you sure you have everything?" I asked cheerily.

A cold "No" was his reply. His curt responses became irksome, a reminder that this was the best thing for both of us. New beginnings are always frightening, but on the other side of fear is freedom. As expected, the painfully long ride from Silverlake to LAX was fraught with endless rush-hour traffic. Outside of a few angry road rage curse words on my part, all was quiet on the western front.

Peter's flight to Amsterdam took place on September 10, 2001—I repeat, SEPTEMBER TENTH, TWO THOUSAND ONE—so getting into the airport was a breeze. I pulled up to the Tom Bradley International Terminal and maneuvered through the chaos of screaming families carting tons of crap home to their third-world countries. I arranged for a porter to help Peter through check-in, and we stood in front of each other, stoic, then bear-hugged ever so tightly.

This was "goodbye," not "see you later." He turned to follow the porter into the terminal, and I continued to look at him as he walked away. "Yoo-hoo!" I yodeled. He spun around, I waved for him to return, and he looked at me inquisitively. I knew he had less cash on him than he cared to admit, so I slipped three hundred dollars into his pocket and kissed him on the cheek. "I love you," I said, not lying. I still loved him—I just didn't like him anymore.

On the lonely ride home to Silverlake, I felt unexpectedly relieved. Woodstock and Alfie shot me a curious look. I pulled a couple of treats from my pocket. If only I could be a dog in my next life, preferably a miniature French poodle in a Jewish American Princess' household somewhere in a warm climate. They get everything they need, enjoy being fawned over, and don't have jobs.

When I returned home from the airport, I was numb. The house was so quiet. An eerie silence blanketed the LA Basin like in Stephen King's book, *The Stand,* after a catastrophic plague has killed off much of the world. Stillness. No sirens, no cars honking, no helicopters hovering, no dogs barking from neighboring homes. Yet, calamity was in the air, the calm before a storm. I'd taken a punch in the gut and wondered if I'd be alone forever. I'll never forget that day, September 10, 2001, when my earth stood still. I got into bed, tried to read, tried to write, and tried to watch *The Sopranos*, these petty, murdering goombahs. What were we glamorizing? What has become of our culture? Nothing made sense anymore.

I finally dozed off and was woken by the phone ringing at six in the morning. It was Peter, no doubt, telling me that he'd landed safely. I hesitated because I wasn't ready to talk to him, but I quickly grabbed the phone.

"Turn on the TV," Peter insisted in a tone of urgency that I'd never heard in his voice.

"What? What time is it?"

"Just please turn on the TV," he cried. "Hurry, you won't believe it."

Annoyed, I patted down my duvet, looking for the remote, which is one of God's little cruel jokes, as I'm forever looking for that damn thing, even when it's inches away from me. I clicked on CNN to see the devastation in progress. The first of the Twin Towers was engulfed in flames—was I watching a movie? The anchor was using the word *terrorism* or perhaps a misdirected Cessna. But that couldn't possibly have been the case; it'd be like a dragonfly knocking over an oak tree.

"Oh, my fucking God." I, too, burst into tears imagining the horror of being in those buildings. We stayed on the call in silence, whimpering, horrified. Suddenly, we saw a long shot of another plane hitting the second tower, and the horror that changed the world forever officially happened. We screamed. The evildoers had done the unthinkable. They had waged a war on the United States. It was Pearl Harbor all over again. Hate and fury were taking over the hearts and minds of the world. Loss was suddenly the common thread that bound us. As Tower Two collapsed, the tears had become unstoppable, and I had to hang up to call my family and hear their reassuring voices. After knowing the Gurko clan was safe, I called Lily to prepare her for what had happened. Surely, work would be suspended today. I was left alone with my thoughts in Silverlake with the dogs to comfort me. Peter was gone. People were dead. World War III loomed, and all was not right in the world. And it wouldn't be for some time to come.

Throughout the day, I, like the rest of the world, stayed glued to the TV screen, waiting to get any news and increasingly shocked at the reports coming from New York City.

Being a displaced New Yorker, I got an odd sense of comfort from calling friends back east to get their "Where were you the moment the towers were hit?" stories. Public grief is intense. People need to communicate and share. Loss and helplessness have a profound impact on how we process feelings. Having just lost the love of my life—well,-my longest-term relationship, anyway—had somehow put me in sync with those who had just lost loved ones. No, no, no, not for a second am I comparing the level of pain and suffering of those directly impacted by 9/11 to the end of my romance. But loss is loss. Going through the stages of grief is a common thread that human beings share. Heartbreak just is, and we each process it differently—in our own way and time. There is no right or wrong about our feelings.

Work was canceled for a few days, and Peter and I frantically called each other. I began to doubt what the hell we had just done. If life was short, did I really want to spend my last days on Earth at the beck and call of an entitled celebrity, especially with all the pride swallowing required to get through any given day? Suddenly, my job, which I had enjoyed, seemed meaningless, and everyone in Hollywood was nothing but a bunch of bloviating, self-involved creatures that offered nothing of interest or value besides their preconceived notions of themselves based on a system that had been created where the talent is trained to believe that they are above everyone else. I'll bet Osama Bin Laden doesn't think that highly of them. A true test of their importance would be whether or not he would bomb something, anything, in Beverly Hills next. As I saw it, no way was that going to happen. He didn't give two shits about Tom Cruise, Gwyneth Paltrow, the Paramount lot, or Rodeo Drive.

Alas, as I predicted, the egomaniacs in Hollywood were convinced that Osama Bin Laden was going to attack LA next, so getting onto the Paramount lot was a nightmare. Every inch of every car was inspected. Getting into the studio for meetings would take up to an hour and a half. I told Peter that night, "Osama Bin Laden doesn't care about Hollywood; what's he gonna do, bomb the Playboy Mansion?" The next few weeks were excruciating as celebrities, their handlers, and assorted Hollywood types were fretting, "We're next." These people with their egos were (and still are) ridiculous.

Then came the Anthrax Scare, ratcheting up the Boogie Man complex to unprecedented levels of hysteria. Tom Daschle and Patrick Leahy, two Democratic senators, were the initial recipients of anthrax-laden envelopes. Five people died as a result of the Anthrax Scare. Mysterious packages were being randomly mailed to government buildings and news stations. Surely, several studio executives must have been upset about not being targeted because it meant missing out on the global attention they so desperately craved.

It was like living through the Summer of Sam in 1978, when Jessie and I would walk home from Studio 54 knowing he was out there somewhere. Now, everyone in the world was experiencing that same dreadful feeling. The terrorists were winning. We were under attack in the most abstract way. 9/11, the Anthrax Scare, and the Internet became a place to recruit willing terrorists, causing the landscape of war to change drastically. With America being the newest battlefield, dealing with unprecedented levels of Hollywood vapidity felt like a waste of time. When all the big talent agencies sent out secret messages to their top-tier celebrity clients addressing their secret stash of CIPRO and reassuring them that all the precious A-list talent would be safe. Not their chores whores, mind you, just "the talent," and I use that term loosely. It was time to get the fuck out of Dodge. Hollywood with all its pomposity could kiss my ass goodbye and point me toward tomorrow.

By November, I called Peter to say I was leaving LA and moving back to NYC. He was still stranded in Amsterdam because the 0-1

Visas were not being re-issued until further notice. We were fighting a new kind of war, a war of wits, and Americans were not winning. The only "MISSION" that George Bush "ACCOMPLISHED" was convincing me to leave the United States, because being back in New York City was no bargain either. Just when I had thought LA was unbearable with its wannabe terrorist attack complex, New Yorkers had gone completely bonkers from the emotional fallout of the actual attack. Peter and I decided that life was short, I would join him in Amsterdam, and we would take our lives one day at a time.

SIDEBAR: Life in Amsterdam was freeing and joyous. However, in short order, our new togetherness reignited our awareness of why we had decided to split in the first place. Once we settled back into that friends WITHOUT benefits thing, it was easy to blame Osama bin Laden for not only devastating the lives of millions of people all over the world, but more importantly, for destroying my sex life. FUCK YOU, OSAMA

FIFTY

So here it was, the eve of turning fifty years old, the dreaded age when my father had drawn his last breath, as had his father before him. Lord knows how far back that horrendous legacy stretches between Poland and Russia and the Pogroms, oh my! The Communists weren't quite as efficient as the Nazis in their record-keeping, so the roots of our family tree are sketchy at best. I had spent my entire adult life expecting to carry on the tragic Gurko tradition of dying young. Let's face it: life is a series of chance encounters with death.

The Santa Ana winds were blowing feverishly, delaying my flight from LA back home to New York. Home? Is that what I was calling New York...again?

SIDEBAR: After living in Los Angeles for a few years, I was asked if I would ever move back to New York. My response was, "I'll move back when it's done." Which meant never, because you know what they say: "Never say never."

I'd been feeling like a foreigner since my return from Amsterdam, having enjoyed a two-year hiatus or midlife crisis—call it what you will. The Manhattan Shuffle takes a lot of energy to reengage in, so I zipped out to LA to see if I could pick up where I had left off there. However, Hollywood isn't an easy reentry either. Out of sight, out of mind, fresh faces or fresh meat preferred.

The polyester bristle of the airplane seat scratched at my very last nerve. I was annoyed being on a red-eye, and there was no one I could be angry with except myself, the worst kind of angry to be. There is nothing romantic about arriving in New York City at the crack of dawn feeling like shit. And anyone who says the red eye is perfect because they can sleep the whole way and feel fresh when they land is lying. As hesitant as I felt about going back to New York, the truth was that there was nowhere else for me to go. I couldn't stay in LA at that time. Unless you were within two degrees of separation from Nicole Richie, you didn't matter. Bloggers ruled, and social media climbing had become a sport. All the fine young cannibals ruled the media. Something was terribly wrong with this picture, and vapidity became the ideal. It paved the way for the Kardashianizing of our culture (or lack thereof). A travesty was brewing, so I opted for the grit of NYC.

This was already a monstrosity of a year: turning fifty, single, terminally freelance, and needing to lose five pounds… again. Twenty years earlier, I would have simply gotten off the plane and changed my ticket to the next plane taking off. Destination: Abandon.

The sound of "fifty years old" was not music to my ears. In fact, it sounded more like the Emergency Broadcast System's warning: "THIS IS A TEST. THIS IS ONLY A TEST" followed by that loud beeping sound. It was a reminder that I was the same age my father had been when he died. A robust, healthy man, gone in sixty seconds. Not that I was projecting that fate onto myself, but I grew up with the tiniest bird on my shoulder warning of my untimely, inevitable demise. Because of that, all decisions were made with the notion, "Why bother committing to anything? I'm gonna die anyway." Of course, that's no way to live, but I couldn't help thinking about it from time to time. It must be the subconscious reason why I never was never able to finish anything. Unfinished manuscripts in the desk drawers, stacks of mail on the table, piles of vintage clothing that needed altering. Having never started a savings account and ignoring Uncle Sam, I was good at telling others how to live their lives. But, then again, do as I say, not as I do.

Especially today, on the eve of my angst-ridden birthday, was my time running out? I was like a walking improvised explosive device (IED), not knowing if I would kaboom at any moment. I hoped it would be in my sleep as opposed to being splattered to pieces by a runaway truck. Since I hadn't OD'ed on drugs yet, perhaps that wasn't the way I was supposed to go. Perhaps I could hold onto dear life long enough to explode with the rest of the world at the end of the Mayan Calendar on December 21, 2012. At least that gave me a few more years in which to accomplish something of note, something that mattered.

Having skated in and out of AA over the years in the past, I had vowed not to keep alcohol in the house—my version of sobriety. This left me two options for celebrating my birthday. One was to go out for a drink with a friend, but the word "celebrate" wasn't an option. The other choice was to hit the gay bars alone to wallow in my impending demise. Neither felt like a win. What to wear that was both slenderizing and youthful? Vivian always said, "The Gurkos look better in black."

As I approached Barracuda Bar, my cell phone rang. It was my friend Myra, whom I had known since my Studio 54 days when she was the club's publicist. I hadn't seen her for years. She was now on the board of the Savannah Film Festival, knew I had worked in Hollywood, and was calling me in desperation because she needed a last-minute replacement to serve as a judge at the festival. I guess this was a perk to being a Chore Whore—working for a celebrity classified me as a good enough candidate in a pinch.

"Can you leave first thing in the morning?" she begged.

"Of course."

Happy birthday to me, indeed. I slipped the phone into my jacket pocket, took a deep breath, and walked into the bar.

As suspected, I was the oldest creature in the place. My black, weather-beaten motorcycle jacket was surely older than most of the guys there. Thank God Savannah loomed, as it would make for great idle chit-chat should my fear subside long enough to allow me to start a conversation with anyone. In fact, if I played my cards right, the blather about being a judge at a film festival might help me pick up a trick, the best birthday present for the newest member of AARP. Ouch. I noticed a guy across the room staring at me. I wondered if this was innocent cruising or more like in the film *Cruising,* as in targeting his next victim, á la *Looking for Mr. Goodbar.* I mustered up my best John Wayne impression, sidled up to the bar, and ordered a Jack and ginger. I needed a stiff drink to ring in the big Five-Oh!

There I was in a sea of nondescript queens, trying to smile at the person on my left with an awkward half-smile that was ignored, and getting the same response from the guy on my right. I finally got the bartender's attention and he took my order, not once looking me in the eye and barely acknowledging my presence. I took the drink and walked through the crowd, feeling invisible. I remembered why it felt safe to be in a relationship. Even if your partner didn't see or hear you, at least you weren't alone. The guy I initially noticed eyeing me was already deep in conversation with someone else, which was a relief because at least I knew that I wouldn't die by being snuffed out by a murderer. The Invisible Man would probably have had better luck getting picked up around here because he was younger, taller, thinner, and that sinister mask he wore would be a big hit with the fetishists in the crowd.

Remember, I resented being a daddy type and was horrified at the notion that I would be considered a Bear type. Being lumped into a group with men known for being older and larger did not bode well for someone who had spent his life obsessively dieting and moisturizing.

Feeling like a ghost was the last thing I needed. That, coupled with the impending doom of the Gurko half-century milestone, dampened my spirits. The sands of time were sifting through the hourglass, and the end of days loomed just minutes away. I finished my drink and bolted out of the bar to go home and pack for my crack-of-dawn flight. Savannah was an opportunity to forget my troubles, come on, get happy.

Not Scarlett's Savannah

I arrived at Savannah Airport, retrieved my luggage, and went outside for a taxi. I noticed a strange-looking man holding up a sign with my last name on it. He reminded me of Igor, the character Marty Feldman had played in *Young Frankenstein.* I walked toward him, smiling.

"Mr. Gurko?" he garbled.

"That's me."

"Walk this way."

Did he really just say that? I laughed and followed him, hoping he had a limp that, for my own amusement, I could mimic the way Gene Wilder had done in the film. We got into the van, and "Igor" inquired, "Do you know that Savannah is the third-most-haunted city in the world?"

"Is that so?" I sniffed. It sounded as unimpressive as being the Mountain Dew to Coca-Cola and Pepsi.

"Be sure to take the Ghost Tour one night while you're here."

"I live in New York City; nothing really scares me anymore. Have you taken the subway at rush hour? That's enough to scare the bejesus out of any ghost."

"Savannah ghosts are different. They get under your skin. You'll see."

We spent the rest of the ride to the hotel in silence. He was spooky enough.

I arrived at the Marshall House, Savannah's oldest hotel, built in 1851. It had been used as a hospital by the Union Army during the Civil War and on two other occasions during the 19th-century yellow fever epidemics. Countless deaths had taken place there. The bellman opened the car door and said, "Welcome to Marshall House, the most haunted hotel in America."

Now, I'm no mathematician, but if Savannah was the third most haunted city, then wouldn't the hotels in those other places take the top spot for most haunted? Whatever; the spook-marketing campaign for the Savannah Chamber of Commerce was giving me the heebie-jeebies. I approached the concierge, who welcomed me with a warm smile, and before she could spit out some haunted hullabaloo, I said, "I know, I know, haunted hotel, haunted city, blah, blah blah."

She smiled, then shot me a look that said, "You'll see."

The young bellhop showed me to room #418. I noticed him grinning, having overheard my conversation about the haunted nonsense that I'd been accosted with since touching down in Savannah. As I walked into the room to look at the accommodations, he disappeared before I could tip him.

"He's definitely part of the act," I snickered as I unpacked.

The bedroom had a grand king-sized bed, á la the *The Haunting of Hill House*, complete with canopy, massive headboard, and bed skirts. I went into the bathroom to wash up and returned to rest before a scheduled meeting with Myra in the lobby. As I approached the bed, I noticed the bed skirt swaying but thought I must have kicked it, which made no sense, as I wasn't near it yet. I chalked it up to a draft from the air conditioner.

"Whatever, Casper," I muttered, and fell into a deep sleep.

A knock on the door jostled me out of a dream. I got up and asked who it was. No response. I sat back down on the bed and heard another light tap on the door.

"Who is it?"

Annoyed, I went to the door and opened it, finding no one there. I figured the hotel-haunted scam was in full bloom, and they did silly things like hiding after knocking on doors. It was time to go downstairs. At least the ghosts were conscientious about my schedule and had prevented me from oversleeping.

I threw on a black blazer and went to the lobby to meet the people I would be spending the next week with. It included an actor, a director, a producer, a marketing executive, a film professor, a film reviewer, and myself. We reviewed our itineraries, which were jam-packed with films, panel discussions, parties, a gala dinner, and a bit of sightseeing. Guess what was first on our agenda for this evening? The Savannah Ghost Tour.

We took a break after a short while and agreed to meet back in the lobby bar in an hour. I returned to my room and, as a joke, said "Boo" when I walked in. As I entered the bedroom area, I noticed the bed skirts moving. This time I chalked it up to creating a draft when I closed the door, which was too far from the bed to make any sense. Then I thought that it must have been the air conditioning. I went to the thermostat and noticed that the air conditioning was turned off. The light in the bathroom was also off, but I had specifically left it on before going downstairs. I thought perhaps Housekeeping had come in to turn down the bed, and then I realized that the bed had not been turned down yet. I started changing clothes and ignored a tap on the door. I walked out of the dressing area and again noticed the bed skirt moving. I threw on a shirt, took the room key, and went downstairs to the Concierge.

"So, hi, can you tell me about this haunted house thing?"

"Yes, of course, Mr. Gurko. Here's a brochure about The Marshall House's history. When it was used as a hospital, many people died here, and it is said that some of the spirits have not been able to move on. What room are you in?"

"Room 418."

"Oh, yes, that's Gracie. She's a bit of a troublemaker. I can assure you she's harmless."

"Tell me more about Gracie."

"She likes playing hide and seek under the bed and turning lights off."

"Yup, that's her, all right."

"Gracie died from yellow fever when she was barely a teenager."

"That's so sad. But is there a room that doesn't have a Gracie that I could switch to?"

"I'm so sorry, Mr. Gurko, but with the festival opening tomorrow, we are way overbooked. I can assure you Gracie is a sweet little girl."

"I don't doubt that, but surely there must be something we can do? Exorcism? Ghostbusters?"

"Here are a few drink passes for the hotel bar. That should help a bit."

"Thanks."

I went to the bar, ordered a shot of tequila, downed it, and went back to my room to see if it was all in my imagination.

"Hello, Gracie. I know you're in here. Looks like we'll be living together for the next week. I'm happy to do that, but I need you to stop playing under the bed."

The lights in the bathroom went out again. "And stop playing with the damn light switches!"

I had to finish changing for the evening's festivities.

"And don't look, either."

I quickly changed and went to the bar to meet up with the other judges. I didn't tell the group about Gracie yet. When we were halfway through the Ghost Tour, I said, "This isn't scary. If you want to see a ghost, come to my room. It's haunted by a spirit named Gracie, a young girl who died of yellow fever."

Naturally, when everyone piled into my room, Gracie remained invisible.

"Come on out, Gracie. Turn off the lights, please. Something. Come on, girl. I want you to meet my new friends."

Nothing. My new friends must have thought, "What a loon." Since we had a big day ahead of us, the gang left me to my seeming insanity. As soon as they left, the bed skirt rustled. "That's not nice; I'm mad at you." I took a sleeping pill, watched some local news, and was awoken by a knock on the door at the crack of dawn. Again, no one was there, and this was becoming less scary and far more annoying.

"Tell your friends never to interrupt my sleep again."

I went under the sheets and pulled the covers over my head.

When the alarm clock rang, I leaned over the bed to see if my roommate was awake yet and called room service to deliver a large pot of coffee with an extra glass of milk in case Gracie was thirsty. I stared at the ceiling and thought that maybe this Gracie obsession existed only in my head and the hotel marketing department had somehow rigged the room. Surely, testimonials were key to keeping the scam of "First Hotel or Third Most Haunted City in America" alive. This was before Yelp.

I got up to shower quickly and covered my genitals in case Gracie was real; far be it from me to be a pervert. While waiting for the coffee, I began reading about ghosts online and was intrigued by a passage that said, "Some spirits may be waiting for a trigger or an event of some kind to occur before they can move on. In some cases, if we are able to figure it out, we may be able to help them."

That reminded me of an obscure Abbott and Costello movie I loved called *The Time of Their Lives.* It starts during the Revolutionary War when two people are wrongly accused of being traitors and shot, condemning their spirits to be trapped in the house that George Washington was supposed to come to at the onset of the war. Their spirits are bound to the house until they're proven innocent, which would allow them to move on. There is a letter hidden in a clock that proves their innocence, which ultimately gets discovered hundreds of years later when a new family moves into the house, finds the letter, and finally frees the two spirits.

Remembering that film gave me the idea to embark on a meaningful project, which was to try to figure out how I could help Gracie move on to her next realm. And hopefully sooner rather than later, in case I might be so lucky as to have the opportunity to bring a trick back to the hotel room while I was in the throes of VIP film festival judge treatment. Being a judge at a movie festival with countless wannabees buzzing around was as good as it gets for my ego.

Between films and panel discussions, I went to the Savannah Public Library to research the Yellow Fever of 1876. The statistics were upsetting. It had happened before physicians knew that mosquitoes transmitted the dreaded disease. Due to poor sanitary conditions that politicians ignored, sixteen heavy days of non-stop rain created swampy areas where mosquitoes and disease thrived. In total, over 1,000 people died that year of yellow fever.

Researching Gracie was another matter entirely. It was hard to pinpoint who she might have been. Nothing mattered to me more than wanting to free her spirit. I had experienced the feeling of being invisible, and it increased my motivation to help her. The thought of being stuck in a place of unhappiness in my afterlife compelled me to want nothing more than to save her. Although being a judge at a festival came with the joy of being treated like a celebrity, somehow it felt meaningless compared with easing the plight of Gracie who deserved the freedom to move on. In the process of helping her, maybe I could conquer a few demons of my own.

Each night, I had another encounter with Gracie. I chose to maintain a dialogue with her, hoping she could understand that I wanted to help her. I hoped she would show me a sign that would help me figure out how to help her. Perhaps her playful actions were, in fact, hints that she was giving me, and I simply wasn't connecting the dots. Hiding under the bed, turning off lights—what situations cause people to do that? What could that mean, if anything? Was she trying to tell me something?

One evening, the group of judges went to the iconic Wall's Barbeque. Afterward, we toured the famous Bonaventure Cemetery that was featured in that horrible film based on the excellent book, *Midnight in the Garden of Good and Evil*. We walked through the gardens where, lo and behold, I was shocked to see a huge statue of a little girl sitting in a chair that read, "Gracie."

Naturally, I imagined that this was her gravesite and wondered if it was she who inhabited my room. As I delved further into the story, things didn't match what the concierge had said. When I returned to the hotel, I questioned the night manager.

"I was told that Little Gracie in Room 418 died of yellow fever, but there happens to be a Little Gracie statue at the Bonaventure for a girl who died of pneumonia."

"And your question is?"

"Is it possible they are one and the same?

"Sir, I hardly believe anyone can confirm that story."

"I was hoping to get some answers because, because, oh, never mind."

I stormed up to my room.

"Gracie, appear, I need to talk to you. I'm serious, not playing." I ordered.

The bed skirt moved. I imagined a little girl in a white dress.

"Look, sweetie, I am going to help you leave this place so you and I can finally rest. Now, I know you can't talk to me, but please just listen. I know what it feels like to be invisible. It's hard to explain why I do. I just do. And it's an awful feeling. Sometimes we do and say things to people just so they will see us. And the truth is, we shouldn't have to do that. People should see us for who we are, and we shouldn't bother with those who don't. I really want to see you, and I think I do see you in my head."

I felt tears welling up. I was talking to my younger, fat, four-eyed self.

"And I know you want me to see you. That's why you're always teasing me. You must believe me; I want to take you out of here so you don't have to stay here at the hotel anymore, all by yourself."

Whether it looked like I was talking to myself or a wall didn't matter. I wanted to take Gracie to the Bonaventure and show her the statue. The bed skirt stopped moving.

"Gracie, come with me. I'm taking you for a walk."

I opened the door, turned, and said, "Come on, it's okay. Just come with me."

I wanted to believe she was real and up for the task. I held the door for her, imagining this sweet kid leaving the place where she had been bound for centuries. I took the stairs since she probably didn't know what an elevator was, and it could look kind of spooky if you think about it. Marshall House had only four floors, and as we walked down the stairs, I felt brisk, cold pockets of air when, again, there was no air conditioning since it was almost November. I imagined it was one of Gracie's ghost friends saying hello.

We walked through the lobby. I talked to Gracie, and people looked at me like I was nuts talking to myself, but I didn't care. "I'm doing the work of a clairvoyant. Get out of my way," I thought. Halloween decorations were everywhere, as this was All Hallow's Eve, a.k.a. Mischief Night, appropriately named.

"Gracie, take my hand."

I stretched out my hand as we passed a group of loud teenagers acting mischievous. I laughed because they looked at me like I was some kind of kook. I felt a sensation in my hand and thought to myself, "Nah."

But who knows? Right? If you can believe in miracles, why not ghosts? Who's to deny anyone's belief system? The important thing is to believe in yourself, or is it myself, which I was beginning to understand from doing this exercise of taking Gracie to the Bonaventure.

We arrived at the cemetery, and I said, "Don't be afraid. These are your friends and family." Maybe I was getting carried away, but to hell with it. I was all in on the mission to free Gracie's soul and mine in the bargain.

We arrived at the statue, and a brisk wind blew through the cemetery. If a wolf howled, I might freak out, but otherwise, this was what I was hoping for. A sign that Gracie at least knew that she could stay here for eternity. Whether this was the same Gracie or not, I was eager to believe it was.

"Well, kiddo. We can go back now. I just thought you should see your options besides under my bed in Room 418."

As we walked back to the hotel, we passed a dress shop, and like a good gay uncle, I stopped to show her the latest styles in the window.

The ice cream shop next door was open, and I decided to get a vanilla cone and ate it in a way that implied she could have a taste. Okay, maybe I was completely nuts, but who isn't?

Back at the hotel, I got into bed, said, "Goodnight, Gracie," and smiled, thinking of George Burns. I tried to imagine how awful it would feel to be trapped somewhere for eternity. I believed in reincarnation; I was convinced I would come back in my next life as a beautiful blonde woman with big tits. I wanted to save the future me from what was my greatest fear: Being trapped as my old self in New Jersey, God forbid.

The whole Gracie experience was really me talking to a much younger me. Feeling invisible was my own doing. I didn't need to be seen by anyone who didn't want to see me. I needed to see myself as a good person and stop looking for validation from people whose attention would make me feel whole. I needed to move on from those feelings of loneliness and turn that energy internally toward loving myself. Besides, feeling invisible did not make me look thinner.

The last night of the festival fell fittingly on Halloween. You can imagine the madness that ensues in Savannah on that particular night. The seven of us judges got good and drunk along with the cast and the director of the festival's Best Film winner. We wound up at the hotel bar where I confided to the group about my Gracie mission that I had kept from them after that first night. I told them what had happened.

Someone had the brilliant idea to throw Gracie a goodbye party. We all piled into the elevator, drinks in hand, and decided to have a séance. Since we were tipsy as hell, we couldn't stop giggling, but we were obviously having a blast and suddenly the bed skirt moved and Gracie joined the party after all. Everyone played along. I imagined her having the much-needed birthday party she had been denied, year after year, since her untimely death.

What happened at the Marshall House with Gracie revived my spirit, no pun intended. She gave me hope that I could meet the challenge of aging gracefully in New York City and find a modicum of joy and the freedom to live my best life.

GOD'S LOVE WE DELIVERED

Starting fresh at fifty takes the kind of gumption that built America. I moved into a friend's sublet on the Upper West Side and took a freelance gig at a photo studio producing fashion nonsense. Someone at work mentioned volunteering for an organization that needed people in their events department. Bingo. If you have ever worked for an A-list celebrity, then you can easily segue into the events business because every day is a special event. Depending on how needy the celebrity was (as in my case, very), this gig would be a cakewalk.

"What's the name of it?" I asked.

"God's Love We Deliver."

Excuse me? Did she say *God*, as in Dear God? That God? I wondered.

"So many fun people volunteer there, too," she added. "It's like a soup kitchen that delivers. But only to people who are homebound, living with AIDS, and too sick to cook for themselves."

My heart sank. "When are you going there next? Can I come?"

"People clamor to volunteer there. You have to sign up for a shift in the kitchen."

"Kitchen?"

"Everyone who's anyone is in that. It's the only place. You should check it out." She told me she would add my name to her next shift, and we would go together.

A few days later, we went uptown to the kitchen in the basement of a youth hostel near Harlem to chop carrots—hundreds upon hundreds of carrots. The woman beside me, Kay, quietly chopping away, was the Director of Development, a refugee from the fashion industry. We began chatting and found that we had much in common and many mutual acquaintances. (Notice how I didn't say *friends*?) She recognized my kindred spirit, and we reminisced about Studio 54, where our paths had most likely crossed. She said she had barely kept in touch with her old friends from back in the day.

"The word *friends* gets bandied about too frequently," I said, telling Kay about my recent Hollywood shuffle. "It's a whole lotta hullabaloo," I added, and she agreed wholeheartedly. Kay invited me to interview for a position on the events team, and within a week, I was God's Love We Deliver-ing.

Part of the gig was that we had to do a shift a week in the kitchen, which was a blast. Every day, there was a different lineup: a parade of Fifth Avenue swans, singers, actors, and politicians. Chopping veggies for three hours became a freeing, moving experience that would be hard to describe, coupled with the fabulous people-watching. Cooking with gas for a great cause. It was a double whammy: raising money to do God's work and helping people who could very easily have been me had I not taken control of my health. I occasionally volunteered to deliver meals, which was intense and rewarding, though difficult. Most times, the God's Love delivery person was the only human connection the client had that day, since too often, their families and friends had abandoned them. Sometimes I'd stay to chat with them even though it was heartbreaking to notice how much they reminded me of the images of people in concentration camps that I had become way too familiar with. This had me wondering how often survival comes down to the luck of the draw. How much control do we have over our destinies? Why was I lucky? Why were my parents lucky? What a catastrophe that the lives of these once beautiful, vital people had been utterly shattered.

The God's Love gig was groovy in a way that was totally different from my experience in La La Land because Wonderland was not always so wondrous. The people on the New York charity circuit were genuinely altruistic. Some could be nauseatingly pretentious, but Hollywood had prepared me for every level of phony baloney.

Dear God,
Boy, is there a lot to chew on here or what? Is it possible that
I'm happy? Should I expect a shoe to drop? I don't see any
Nazis on the horizon. How random to wind up at God's Love,
of all places. Your Love, doing your work? Can I take this
moment of joy as a sign? You better not be fucking with me.
Love,
ABE

The "angel" of God's Love was Blaine Trump, the sister-in-law of that Gross Baboon, Donald. Blaine and her elegant patron swans towered over the rest of the Trump family. She was not a tacky hanger-on like The Donald, as he preferred to be called (feel free to throw up). It should be no surprise that Donald's immediate family were not known for their philanthropy back in the day, and nothing's changed since then. Meanwhile, the stunning Blaine was the doyenne of fabulosity. She was nothing like Donald's slags—I mean, wives. Her network was legendary, as was her integrity. When she first read about the lifesaving work of God's Love in the *Times*, Blaine—elegant as a gazelle—pranced up to the 103rd Street and Amsterdam Avenue basement kitchen, knocked on the door, and said, "I want to help." And help she did. Blaine single-handedly made God's Love the premiere charity on which New Yorkers wanted to shower their time and resources. As the need for meals outgrew the basement kitchen, David Geffen donated a building in Soho to serve as the new downtown headquarters. And away we went, lock, stock, and bagel.

SIDEBAR: Donald always seemed envious of Blaine because she was everything he could never be, as well as the toast of the town. He would show up at our events and try to steal Blaine's thunder, to no avail. The media loved her and could barely stomach him. Having stood way too close to that big blob of stink, I had to hold my breath—one of my many talents from the fitness training days—at the stench of his cheap cologne. God's Love staff never kowtowed to that (current) loser. It was always Team Blaine with her bevy of fabulous "ladies who lunch" who spent time in the kitchen, including Martha Stewart, Anna Wintour, Naomi Campbell, and Lynda Carter, to name a few.

Naturally, I had to move downtown as well because the beauty of New York City is creating a world where you can walk to and from work, preferably through neighborhoods that have charm and character—quintessential city living. I had to give up on Soho as the rents were skyrocketing and living south of 23rd Street was hugely desirable. When real estate brokers figured out how many millions of dollars they could siphon off of hipsters by renovating those incredible cast iron buildings, you do the math. I couldn't afford to live there. Apartment hunting for a good or even decent apartment in NYC is not for the faint of heart. It's war. You are at the mercy of heartless landlords and brokers who drag you on countless viewings of shitholes where rats wouldn't live, schlepping up countless flights of stairs, even though you've sworn to never look above a parlor floor. Those cunning agents know what words to use to tempt you to drag your sorry ass up, up, up even more stairs, holding onto creaking banisters for dear life. The longer you live in Manhattan, the more likely you are to have been through this rigamarole.

As luck would have it, I wandered through the Meatpacking District after having dinner at Florent, one of the few late-night places in the city that served food after the bars and clubs let out. There was nothing like Florent's vintage-style diner after 4 AM. He was the mastress-of-ceremony of the downtown scene, overseeing his clinking, clanking court of caliginous drunkards and druggies. I jotted down the phone numbers of neighboring buildings. The area smelled of rotting meat and cheap perfume. I knew I wanted to make this my home. The Meatpacking District was primarily meatpackers and transgender sex workers. Chasing down leads, I cornered a guy whose dad owned several buildings in the area. Daryl is a third-generation descendant of meatpackers who bought land when it was dirt cheap, making him a member of the uber-lucky sperm club. Figuring he was on the take, I offered him cash under the table so Daddy wouldn't know, and he offered me a groovy zone for peanuts since, late at night, the neighborhood was shady at best. Several weeks after I moved in, *New York Magazine* published a cover story titled

"The Wild West—Can Lawyers and Club Kids and Drag Queens and Butchers Find Happiness Together in Manhattan's Meatpacking District?" That "get" was God working in my life again, for sure.

As I settled into my new life back on the East Coast, I was happy to reconnect with my family, the three women who would always inhabit the biggest piece of my heart. We resumed the warmth that was our family's modus operandi. My sisters and I enjoyed a weekly three-way call on Saturday nights. We were all single at that time and shared many giggles. It felt good to be back in the Gurko pocket, feet firmly planted on the ground, willing to throw a few seeds to see what might grow. My spiritual journey has taught me that all we have is today, and when you embrace that, all is well in the world. God really did deliver.

THE GAY DIVORCEE

The art of gay weddings had not yet begun to litter the "Sunday Style" section of *The New York Times* when I attended my first gay wedding in Montecito, California, during the summer of 2000. It was a poetic affair held at a grand, sprawling Gilded Age estate owned by a friend who was in real estate and considered a magician at flipping the most exclusive properties in Southern California. While updating one of those palatial digs, he made it the venue for his wedding to a queen he had met online. By coincidence, I had tricked with his future betrothed years earlier when I lived in New York City back when he had more hair and was fifteen pounds lighter. But far be it from me to sound like a bitchy queen. I don't know about your experience with online dating, but heat-seeking for true romance by trolling the Internet's M4M chat rooms rarely makes for happily-ever-after endings. This was before the triumphant, soul-crushing rise of online dating services like Match, eHarmony, and Grindr.

The wedding was an overtly spiritual affair with one hundred of the couple's best-est-est friends in attendance sipping Negronis. We nibbled on lovely caviar and smoked salmon canapés, real crab cocktail parfaits, and avocado toast rounds. Limoncello shots were passed as the sun set over the Pacific Ocean. The mountains of Montecito must be the "purple mountains' majesty" that we sing about in "America the Beautiful." Love was in the air, especially after three Negronis and two Limoncello shots.

A triangular dinner bell rang, summoning the guests to assemble for the "symbolic" sunset ceremony about to begin. On the spacious front lawn, we formed a large circle as the groom and groom went from guest to guest, one by one, face to face, with searing eye contact, whispering to each of us why we were so unique in their lives and that they loved us. I was standing next to one of the stars of *The Sopranos,* Tony's sister. We had connected during the cocktail hour—she was another true, sarcastic New Yorker with the magnetic pull that exists therein. She hinted, sipping on Negronis, that it seemed odd the wedding was happening so unexpectedly. She had been friends with Monty since before he made his first million.

"We know it's not a shotgun wedding," she said, smirking, libations kicking in. "They live on different coasts?"

"Citizenship?" I offered, usually being right.

"I didn't even think of that."

"Who knows what goes on behind closed doors?" I dared not say I had known him biblically.

As the two grooms came close enough for us to smell their freshly rosewater-bathed bodies, she side-eyed me, and we choked back the giggles.

The cocktails had taken effect, and we tried—to no avail—to refrain from laughing out loud as they approached us full frontal. The more politically correct types in the circle began giving us dirty looks, but we couldn't hold back the tears and finally burst out laughing. That triggered a chain reaction of snickering and snorting until this painfully confrontational love fest ended. Otherwise, the evening was lovely, as hokey as it was.

An elegant dinner was served while Pachelbel's Canon in D Major serenaded us as we took our seats at two long, intersecting tables. Like a cross. Yes, that cross.

SIDEBAR: Keep in mind, gay weddings, especially on this grand scale, were not yet a thing. Expectations ran sky high for how queens would set the stage and redefine the wedding milieu. Everything would have to be spectacular. Venue? Incredible. Flowers? Magnificent. Food? Move over, Martha Stewart. Wedding March? Pachelbel's Canon in D Major. WHAT?

I grabbed my Soprano's arm and whispered how lame that song choice was. "This is the official wedding march for all straight, white people. They couldn't have bumped it up a coupla centuries?"

She spat out her drink and said, "It's also the song in *Ordinary People* when that girl kills herself."

We both burst out in hysterics. At that exact moment, the two well-groomed grooms were trying to shush us, standing at the head of the cross-shaped table, solemnly gazing into each other's eyes and spewing nonsense.

"This cross represents the intersectionality of our union, bringing us together with people we love. The act of breaking bread, and like Jesus, we want to share our love and bare our souls." Yada...yada...I can't...you can imagine the rest.

I thought I would pee my pants. We were getting the evil eye from all sides and choked back the giggles with more booze. Glasses of Veuve Clicquot Brut were raised to toast the happy couple, followed by disco dancing under the stars and the full moon. They had thought of everything. We danced till the sun rose and were treated to a sumptuous breakfast picnic. L'amour, l'amour.

Six months to the day after, I went to my first gay divorce at the same estate. The property was not selling, creating financial hardships for the not-so-happy couple. My ex-trick, soon-to-be an ex-husband, had already moved back to New York. It wasn't quite the same joyous occasion, but plenty of snarky one-liners led to many giggles. A baker's dozen of us who had attended the nuptials came back to sit Matrimonial Shiva, as it were. We spent the evening pawing through legal documents, trying to find a loophole so he could get out of paying alimony. We drank whiskey and ordered Chinese takeout and finally found the key sentence that got him out of paying "that schmuck" alimony. Now, finally, he could live happily ever after.

Since I'm not a betting man, having lost my shirt at nineteen years old on a vacation in the Bahamas (a long story for another time), I would not bet my life that I will live "happily ever after" with only one person. What does that expression even mean? Living happily ever after for me would be living for eternity, defying mortality, like a vampire. Happily or otherwise is secondary to wanting to live "ever after." And if "happily ever after" only means "till death do us part," well, that's depressing. I vote to change it to "till death do us party."

Having survived an seven-year relationship, I propose we establish an official "The Party's Over" Party where you gather friends, including the ones you excommunicated for warning you against the union in the first place. You can decorate with "I Told You So" balloons and play silly games to lighten the mood while drinking lovely digestifs and nibbling on small just desserts. The party would celebrate a rite of passage and serve as a kickoff to reclaiming your independence. Call it an after-shit-show celebration or whatever you want. A marching band would seem appropriate, too. If only every life lesson ended with a parade of some sort.

That night, I thought about how silly Monty's marriage was from the jump, and I vowed that if I ever were to find love again, I wouldn't go through that pretentious rigamarole. I thought back to when we bravely fought for our gay rights and the freedom to be ourselves in the '70s. Weddings and inevitable divorces were not even on the Bingo card. This couple represented the new gay community that was losing its edge. Yes, I guess in hindsight, we had marched so that these kids could have the freedom to float in Speedos down Pride parades, get married and divorced, and do every other nonsensical thing that straight people do. Was I becoming a prude in my middle age? Maybe, maybe not. Either way, the times were changing. I was proud to have been part of that initial push to establish the pride movement and even prouder to say, "I am homosexual, yes; gay, no."

YOU TOO CAN BE A GAY DIVORCEE

You still haven't congratulated me for surviving the tumultuous ending of an seven-year relationship, coming out of it feeling like a pro, and having learned yet another harrowing life lesson: the joy of staying single. Coupling endings are never easy; in fact, they're usually very messy, so naturally, that made me the perfect candidate to become a contributor to a newly established online community of divorcees, Divorce Candy dot com. With the divorce rate at an all-time high, a gaggle of well-intentioned marketing mavens knew they could tempt the many newly broken-hearted refugees from connubial bliss (or misery) by creating a go-to website as a much-needed resource. My expertise as "a gay" was sought out to speak to the new crop of gay divorcees who were also suffering from post-coital dysphoria and in need of practical tips and guidance as they journeyed to becoming "The New You."

I had started a blog shortly after the economy crashed in 2008 called "I Mean…What?!? dot com." Divorce Candy got wind of it and learned what an opinionated maven regarding all areas of style and wellness I had become and offered me an advice column because most male divorcees needed a complete overhaul from top to bottom, inside and out. I'd been tasked to shepherd needy, lonely men through the process of revamping their images with tips on grooming, shape-shifting, and other areas of their lives that needed *zhuzhing*. The end of my long-term relationship would be good to reference, and I could share personal stories. My recent experience in Montecito would be perfect fodder for what not to do should you decide to give marriage another go. Someone needed to dictate to this group of newly crushed hopefuls how to live their new lives one day at a time, just like me.

First things first: I am a firm believer in the power of a makeover. When you're newly divorced, there are two ways to tackle the next phase of your life. One is with tremendous optimism and willingness to try new things. The other involves retreating from social activities and allowing self-doubt and trepidation to keep you from moving forward. The latter is probably more familiar because transitioning back to being single again is not easy. You are entitled to wallow in your grief, but self-pity must stop because we have better things to do, like revamp your image and go shopping!

Without question, I am the best candidate to be the Pied Piper to these pathetic people on their new paths to self-improvement. Of course, I am the perfect mentor in all areas of upgrading your life, spiritually and physically. I've done all of the above more than once. Since we are all works in progress, it would be great to lead these people through the initial stages of fear and sadness that come with loss. I have broken down the makeover process into simple steps to follow. Bottom line: An image upgrade is an exercise in self-love and can be a joyous experience.

STEP 1:

Strip off your clothes and stand in front of a full-length mirror. As uncomfortable as this might feel, accepting who you are and what needs some work is critical.

(You might recall the Ides of March 1973, when I did this and never looked back.)

STEP 2:

Move closer to the mirror and stare into your own eyes. It feels awkward, but you must look deep within your soul for the strength to carry on with confidence based on your deductions from Step 1 about what aspects of your appearance will require some tweaking or overhauling.

STEP 3:

Make a to do list. This was mine:

- Get back to the gym, no matter whether you need to lose 5 or 50 pounds. Diet and exercise plans are available through private sessions.
- Buy a new jacket or coat. A great outer layer is an excellent first purchase to add to your wardrobe. Personal stylists are available upon request.
- Get a new hairstyle or beard. A new "do" makes a new you.
- For those who wear eyeglasses, invest in a new pair. It's a game-changer.

You may also need therapy. Correction: You definitely need therapy, and this is where I sign off.

GOD'S LITTLE ACCIDENTS

By the summer of 2012, I was at the top of my game in New York City, thanks to God's Love, the people I met, and the access it provided. I had built up a fabulous portfolio of clients and produced countless high-profile events on both coasts and beyond. I produced fashion shows, music videos, fundraisers galore, art and design industry schmoozefests, and even a 5K charity race in Central Park. You name it, I did it with aplomb à la Edina Monsoon from Ab Fab. My home office in Chelsea was buzzing with fun people, a pot of coffee always brewing, endless chatter and gossip.

MANIFESTO: "Finding truth and humor in a world obsessed with fashion, celebrity, and politics. I Mean…What?!? has become the insider's go-to resource to get a humorous take on the truth about the Emperor's New Clothes, celebrity fashion designers, influencers, and the other absurdities that plague our pop culture landscape."

What started as a fluke, simply rattling off my one-liners into the blogosphere, became popular on both coasts. Was I saving lives? No. Was I happy? Yes. Enjoying a cash flow, relevance, and a feeling of accomplishment felt great. Then life happened.

> SIDEBAR: I'd been conscious of my carbon footprint for years and have been bicycling around New York City since the 1980s. I found the first spin classes, created in LA (naturally) circa 1991 when Johnny G launched his innovative indoor cycling workout program. I was part of his core group as he developed the program, and I became addicted. At that time, I was doing everything to stay healthy, including chugging down gallons of water daily.

SoulCycle had become the rage in New York City, but I didn't like wearing other people's shoes. (That's why bowling had always given me the willies.) Before I took my first SoulCycle class, I ran to buy a pair of cycling shoes at Paragon Sporting Goods en route to the Tribeca studio that fateful Sunday morning. The class started at 11:30 AM. Paragon opened at 11 AM, and I was zooming down to Washington Avenue on my bike when the shopping bag got caught in the spokes of my front wheel and sent me flying. As I was hurtling upside down in what seemed like slow motion, I knew this wasn't going to end well. My left arm and shoulder were mangled. The irony is that I had decided to take the summer off to work on my book—yes, this book. Problem was, I'm a lefty and couldn't write—not even blog posts—so I tried installing a dictation program that somehow screwed up my computer. It started talking to me and wouldn't shut up. Nothing was going right. In fact, this catastrophic accident fell under the header of Alanis Morrissette's song, "Isn't It Ironic," from the album "Jagged Little Pill," which, sadly, I had to start taking for the excruciating pain. Inevitably, I became addicted to opiates.

As the summer slowly rolled by, I lost interest in the upcoming New York Fashion Week or helping to raise funds for anyone. Instead, I focused on healing, which was an excuse for getting more pain medication. I'd lost interest in writing the blog or the book, and of course, my business suffered, my social life suffered, and I was suffering. By Christmas, things were very messy. I'd been doing physical therapy but had not regained full use of my left arm, which was still functioning at only fifty percent of its full capacity.

A healer I'd heard about, Abdi Asadi, whom Norma Kamali swore by, worked his magic and in one session miraculously restored 90 percent use of my arm and shoulder. The thing that didn't heal was my mind and its dependence on the Percocet. The drug had taken its toll. I knew things were bad when I nodded out in a local liquor store and had to be escorted home by a stranger.

Coincidentally and fortunately, my friend Amy came to visit from Los Angeles, took one look at me, and immediately, lovingly insisted that I pack up my dogs, Woodstock and Alfie, and fly to LA to live in her spare apartment smack on Ocean Front Walk in Venice Beach. She offered three months at no charge because she wanted me to clean up my act. In short, Amy was one of my angels. She told me, "You can decide what you want to do by then, but no drugs or alcohol. If I sense anything, you're out that day."

Who doesn't admire a bit of tough love now and again? On January 15, bags and dogs packed, the Chelsea apartment sublet, I was ready to relax and recharge my soul again.

When I landed directly on the beach in this little spot of heaven and watched my first sunset from the apartment, a rush of gratitude felt better than any rush from opiates.

Dear God,
Hallelujah. Thank you for letting me land on my feet again.
I guess you're not ready for me to join you. Hope you're at
least somewhat amused by these little tête-à-têtes we're having
where I am begging you for something, anything, usually my
life. This place feels like heaven, so thank you for Amy and for
the fact that I'm still breathing.
Love,
ABE

The next few months provided an opportunity to reflect on my uncanny ability to meet and survive the challenges thrown in my path. On my first walk along the Venice Boardwalk, I felt transported to 1968 and the Summer of Love, as if time had stood still. This little plot of joy has been featured in countless films and commercials. I wandered into the Small World Bookstore and chose *The Four Agreements, The Artist's Way,* and *Man's Search for Meaning.* I would write a book if it was the last thing I did. Losing my writing arm for months from the bike accident had made it impossible to keep up the momentum and popularity of *I Mean…What?!?* The algorithm of a blog is like a monster that needs to be fed constantly. Everyone and their cousin had started a blog by then, so I didn't mind walking off into the sunset. I'm not a quitter, but I know when to bow out grace-fully instead of hanging on like a television series that continues for too many seasons.

The three months flew by. I wrote a lot, worked out a lot, and contemplated what the fuck to do next. I had escaped the horrendous New York winter, and the thought of returning to a steamy, smelly summer had me rethinking LA. I called Lily, my old LA celebrity boss, and went for a visit. We hadn't seen each other for a few years, but it was as though no time had passed. Lily was one of those people with whom it's effortless to pick up from where you left off, like riding the friendship bicycle. I told her I was thinking of staying in LA. She took my hand and said, "Darling, you are too old and broke to live in New York City. Move in here. You can have the pool house." So I took her up on her offer and moved onto the property, dogs and all.

Dear God,
Thanks. Peace.
ABE

P.S. Sure hope that was the last time I get into trouble. I don't know if I could survive another bout of me being my own worst enemy.

ROMANCING THE STONED

There it was, my beautiful collection of dolls that I'd been painstakingly collecting for what felt like a lifetime. No, not Barbies and Kens and Chrissies. Not Beanie Babies nor Care Bears nor those ridiculous Cabbage Patch Kids nor Trolls and most assuredly not those friggin' Furbys. My idea of dolls was not what millions of little children screamed for at Christmas (or Hanukkah), promising to be nice and not naughty, not realizing that whining fell under the category of the latter.

"Doll" was a word that had various meanings in my life. For instance, I called people "Doll" not as a term of endearment necessarily, but instead because I was the worst at remembering people's names. Faces I never forgot. Names were another matter entirely. Doll, Darling, Stinky. I'd call anyone anything except their actual name. I especially enjoyed addressing straight men with "Hi, Doll," having seduced several straight men in my youth. You never knew who'd be up for the taking. Frankly, I don't care if being called "Doll" makes straight men feel emasculated or uncomfortable, if anything, preferably aroused. That's one of the benefits of living comfortably in your own skin, not giving a damn what anyone thinks. One of my mother's many pearls of wisdom to live by has been, "Who are they to me? What have they done for me?" I guess surviving the Holocaust will give you a bit of an edge.

> SIDEBAR: Who knows? Maybe my doll collecting inadvertently contributed to my inability to remember people's names. Nothing is ever one thing. There's also the little heartbreaking fact that Alzheimer's runs in my family, and dare I say out loud, I might be suffering from a rare case of what one might sadly refer to as "Ridiculously Early Onset Alzheimer's," which then gives my doll collection that much more relevance and power in my life. Confused??? Me too.

Dolls are also what some people—me in particular—call pills. Lovely, delicious pills in a kaleidoscope of colors that had taken me so long to collect since the government crack-down on prescription meds because millions of morons were accidentally overdosing, giving such great pills a bad rap. Neely O'Hara would have approved of my doll collection.

For those of you uncultured types who don't know who I'm talking about, Neely O'Hara was, is, and always will be a drug addict's folkloric hero or antihero. She is one of the three main fictional characters from the wildly popular Jacqueline Susann novel *Valley of the Dolls*. Neely O'Hara, the pill-popping, vodka-swilling bitch sorta became my inspiration at the tender age of eleven. Neely stole my heart. Her character is loosely based on Judy Garland. Need I say more? My kinda gal. *Valley of the Dolls* was THE ultimate bestselling beach read of 1966; everyone was reading it. I had to sneak-read it when my mother wasn't looking because it was considered too "racy" for kids. If you read *Valley of the Dolls* now, you'd see how far down the smut line we have come since the "Summer of Love." Nowadays, sex, drugs, and rock 'n' roll are storylines for television commercials featuring everything from IKEA to Viagra.

Anyway, I would tippy-toe into my parents' bedroom and read one chapter at a time of the forbidden fruit—book, forbidden; me, fruit. *Valley of the Dolls* was my introduction to the adult world of total debauchery, homosexuality, drugs, sex, and suicide—just about all the things I like about life in general. You know the drill when people say, "I loved the book, but the movie was terrible." Well, *Valley of the Dolls* is THE perfect example of that statement. When they announced that a film was going to be made of the notorious trash novel, the hype about who would play Neely O'Hara became the hot topic and kicked off a slutty-mess version of David O. Selznick's worldwide "Search for Scarlett" (O'Hara) for the film *Gone with the Wind*. A massive woman hunt was underway for the lead role of Neely O'Hara. All three lead female roles were highly coveted and, as expected, caused quite a bit of behind-the-scenes drama for that casting. It was leaked to the media that Judy Garland, who had been cast to play Helen Lawson, the oldest addict of the three, was fired for being drunk on set during rehearsals—the hypocrisy of it all. Wasn't Judy just getting into character?

When the word on the street was that Jane Fonda was in the running to play Neely O'Hara, now they were talking. Sadly, Jane also knew how to read and passed on the horrendous script, leaving them with Patty Duke. Patty Duke? One of the most anticipated roles in Hollywood—a drug-addicted singer, dancer, actress, triple threat, and sex addict, based loosely on the riveting life of the incredible Judy Garland—and they gave the role to Patty Duke of Helen Keller fame. The Patty and Cathy goodie-goodie, teenage twins from *The Patty Duke Show* Patty Duke? Really? Somebody give me a pill! It was the risk of the century, and boy, they blew it. To this day, the movie should only be watched for the train wreck that it is.

When the movie came out, I begged and pleaded to see it with my mother. The film opened in Times Square, which was still sleazy and interesting because Rudy Ghoul-iani had not yet ruined Manhattan by turning it into a homogenized Disneyland, replete with the *Lion King, Mary Poppins*, and an M&M Emporium. My mother begrudgingly agreed to take me with her to see the film. What excitement! In the famous scene when Sharon Tate reveals her breasts, nip-slip and all, my mother quickly covered my eyes. If she knew then what we all know now, she wouldn't have bothered.

As for my lovely plethora of pills, there they were, hauntingly calling my name. There's an old black-and-white Edward G. Robinson movie called *Scarlet Street*, where the ghost of the woman he murders drives him into a state of madness and he ends up hanging himself. Hanging is such a weird way to go. And for some odd reason, it seems to be on trend: Mick Jagger's girlfriend, Robin Williams, my niece's ex-father-in-law. Hanging is having a heyday. But hang myself? I'd sooner die, and most assuredly, not that way. It's too violent. No, I am a peace-loving kinda guy who finds solace in excessive pill-taking as a means of sport, but never with the intention to end it all until now.

The good news is that I was convinced that this would not be the end of it all—at all. On the contrary, it would be a new beginning, a new dawn. That's why it's called the afterlife, that which comes after life as we know it. However it manifests, you can still technically call it a life. I was hoping to come back as the Sailor Jerry Pin-Up Girl that I had tattooed on my arm. Imagine, my personality, tall, blonde, with big boobs? That would be a life worth living. Not my so-called life? Not a believer? I sure am now. How do I know this to be true, you may ask in horror and disbelief. I read all about it in the novel *Proof of Heaven* by Dr. Eben Alexander, the brain surgeon who was in a bad accident and journeyed into the afterlife, where his experiences contradicted all of his medical teachings. What better proof do you need? Besides, who hasn't contemplated offing themselves at critical junctures in their life, only to say, "Nah, I love myself too much" or "I'm afraid to die; I want things—as horrible as they are—to stay just the way they are."

The words that Dr. Brain Surgeon used in describing his posthumous experience were so inviting: "Floating, ethereal, intoxicating." Doesn't that sound heavenly, no pun intended? The afterlife sounded slender-izing, too. Plus, no more squeezing into designer jeans and tight little T-shirts, just lots of flowing, white fabric sheaths. What lies beyond life as we know it must be another form of life, no? Even if what that is does not exist, something has to. And if it turns out to be nothingness, how many weekends of doing nothing have you thoroughly enjoyed? Imagine the possibilities of an infinity of that! One for me, two for me, three for me. Let's get this party started. Besides, there can be no such thing as absolute nothingness unless you happen to binge-watch all the seasons of *The Real Housewives of Orange County.*

Am I one hundred percent certain of what awaits us in the great beyond? No one is as optimistic as I am. Hence, that lovely collection of opiates is there to transcend me into my next existence. And frankly, that sounds a lot more interesting than living life on life's terms or being prudent, like Scarlett O'Hara in *Gone with the Wind* when she says, "After all, tomorrow is another day." The proof that wasn't worth a damn is seeing the lame sequel to *Gone with the Wind: Scarlett,* starring Joanne Whalley. I rest my case.

I'm not one of those people who gobbles a whole bottle of pills only to throw them all up. What a waste. My way of doing it—one for me, two for me—lets me enter the next realm with a warm, soothing, floating feeling that opiates provide as opposed to some kind of violent outburst. Can you imagine me hacking at my veins or shooting a handgun at my face? Give me a cozy, opiate-induced coma any day of the week, as it is a much more pleasant way to go. Having made such a big decision and sticking to it was an admirable task. Quite frankly, I had had it with all the years of trying, caring, wanting, hoping, dieting, spinning, denying in the name of wanting, and desperately needing, which was the worst of all. No, my mind was made up. It had taken years of patience to stockpile these fucking pills because good pills were not easy to come by.

As I drifted off to the nether regions of whatever realm I was off to, my life flashed before my eyes. It was that floating sensation I had read about, but it felt more like I was falling and I immediately thought, "Of course, I'm going to hell." What fresh hell was the question. I saw snippets of my life, images of people whose faces I could barely make out. Slow-motion sequences like when Dorothy is on the twister and sees Almira Gulch turning into the witch. As I sank deeper into the darkness, a black-and-white silent movie began flashing in my mind. The stories of my life, in reverse, and hopefully not far back enough to see myself when I was fat.

DETOXING CAN BE SLENDERIZING

Boy, did I wake up with a doozy of a hangover. Guess my time hadn't come— again— yet. As I replayed the evening in my head, remembering the rambling, dangerous nonsense that offers a peek into the mind of a manic addict, it was clear what needed to happen next.

Terrible influences will always present themselves as a test of strength and resistance. Failing is an opportunity to win. It was clear that I needed to, once again, get out of the Dodge I'd been living in, tucked away in the hills of Beverly…swimming pool…movie stars. Living in an idyllic setting can also be deceiving. There was darkness, and I had to flee and find a safe place to land.

The thing about drug addicts is that we swear every time, "This is it, God (beat) damn it." It's the breaking point when you promise never to go down this familiar rabbit hole—correction, hell hole (beat) again. I wasn't expecting God to grant me the serenity, yet again, any time soon. Suffering was on the horizon. I could feel it rearing its ugly head. I was nauseated from jumping off and on this not-so-merry-go-round of addiction. It was getting old, and so was I.

I moved into a West Hollywood apartment with only a mattress and my dogs. The walls in the living room were beveled mirrors, and it could have doubled as a dance studio, but my exertions of energy consisted of breathing, which I was grateful to still be doing. I went to the CVS store around the corner to stock up on the necessities that would sustain me through the inevitable, looming detox, which I was determined to do alone. The idea of being surrounded by whiny addicts at a rehab facility made my skin crawl even more than it was already doing as I entered day two of detox. I didn't want to hear the bumper sticker words of wisdom that the people in the program were so quick to spew: "Easy Does It," "Keep It Simple Stupid," and that heinous chestnut "Let Go and Let God." Thinking back to that horrible day at Bergen Pines, for instinctively not wanting to subject myself to the group psychobabble from people trying to get clean, my inner demon's thoughts were bad enough. Nyquil™, Dayquil™, Theraflu™, vitamins, cranberry and orange juice, Advil™, apples, and lots of chocolate. I was going to survive this self-inflicted pharmaceutical holocaust because I had the best teachers and needed to prove it to them and myself. Comparatively speaking, detox versus Holocaust? Please, girl.

Detoxing from opiates is not for the faint at heart. What Kryptonite is to Superman, opiates were to me. Coping with the debilitating effect of the poison seeping out of the body takes superhuman strength and a super-sized commitment to white-knuckle through the excruciating experience in the hopes of getting to the other side.

This last foray into addiction was a doozy because Fentanyl had entered the picture. The good news—not that the word *good* applies— was that at least the drugs were clean, pharmaceutical grade. My dealer was a legit pharmacist, which convinced my addict brain that it was like getting a prescription from a doctor, with less risk of death.

Following my imaginary doctor's orders, I tried to eat an apple a day. Denial has an insidious way of justifying everything and anything that is not in your best interests. Especially if, like me, you are a functioning addict, where the drugs are so baked into your system that you can handle life, the job, working out, taking care of dogs and people, then crashing every night, while it becomes harder and harder to get out of bed in the morning.

I was disgusted with myself for being so weak and winding up back at square one. I was so sick and tired of being sick and tired from having to pick myself up by my friggin' bootstraps yet again. I could try to lay blame on the people I had chosen to surround myself with, but that would have been a cop-out. "Life is choice." I've always known this and would share my pearls of wisdom with anyone who would listen.

Dear God,
I know, I know. I'm bored with myself, too. I'm not asking
for much this time. Just make sure I live. Lord knows, I have
wandering-Jewed myself around this farshtunkenneh planet
almost to death, but I must survive my own stupidity. If not,
I'll just die, I mean, not literally, hopefully. Please help me,
God, get through this detox, and I promise to the Chumash it
will be the last time or else…I know, I know.
Love,
ABE

I was not prepared for how painful detoxing from opiates would be as the poison oozed out of my body. May you live happily ever after, never knowing the excruciating pain of getting off opiates. Nevertheless, I was determined to go through it alone. My responsibility to my dogs compelled me. Woodstock and Alfie were my heroes. They wouldn't leave my side, as dogs instinctively know when you are sick or sad. God put dogs on Earth because he knew that humans could not survive without them. I know I couldn't. They were the best reasons to get through the next few painstaking, horrific weeks while I clawed my way back to life. For countless hours, I could not move off my bed to take them out, so I just threw wee-wee pads everywhere.

Alfie & Woodstock (RIP), my saviors.

The first few days were unbearable. My body was aching, my brain was exploding, but my spirit compelled me to stay the course. I didn't answer the phone because I was sure to sound like a maimed animal. The pain was excruciating, like being on the rack. After a couple of days, I thought things were getting better, but it was quite the opposite. Crying from pain and fear that I would not survive this ordeal, I couldn't even shower even though I knew it would make me feel better. I couldn't muster the strength to do the simplest things.

The detox nightmares were terrifying; they made my childhood holocaust dreams seem like child's play. It wasn't my mother I was seeing on the inside of the concentration camps. It was me. In one dream in particular, I was being shoved into a gas chamber, trying to scream while no sound came out of my mouth. It felt so real. I woke up in a pool of sweat and so full of rage that I had these two diseases that would plague me for the rest of my life.

I hadn't eaten for a few days, and once I could, I ordered a Chicken in a Pot from Canter's Deli in an effort to chicken soup my soul through detox. Twice a day, I inhaled quarts of soup, which I highly recommend. Then, I finally got a glimpse of my face and was horrified to see a monster in the mirror. As a snake sheds its skin, a few layers of my face cracked off, coupled with red blotches and black circles under my eyes. I hadn't shaved, my eyebrows were out of whack, and hair was coming out of my ears, BUT I was thin, although this time, there was no joy in my '90's heroin-chic look.

Having lived through that nightmare, my takeaway and perhaps my greatest life lesson was not to focus on what led me to the Promised Land but rather appreciate that I got there and survived. Depending on your idea of the Promised Land, one interpretation says it is not an actual place but a catharsis, a sense of inner peace.

Dear, Dear God,
What did I do to deserve your kindness? Thank you, thank
you, thank you for keeping me alive. It won't be for naught.
I am going to make my life matter if it's the last thing I do.
There's got to be some kind of legacy for me to leave behind. In
case, you know, Nazis start marching again. Surely there's a
greater plan in store. I just need a sign.
Love always,
ABE

I CRIED WOLF

Wait…what? Nazis??? Was that a bunch of Nazis I just saw on the news? Talk about days that will live in infamy: August 12, 2017, had friggin' Nazis marching in Charlottesville at their violent Unite the Right Rally. My initial reaction was "Thank God my parents are not alive to see this shit happening here in the United States." After the war, Jews looked to America as a refuge from the tragic events they had endured. And what the fuck was I witnessing? It would be too intense to have a conversation with my parents about this horrendous development in the country they had loved and cherished. The challenge of being a child of Holocaust survivors is that you want to protect them, especially from something like this. As a first-generation U.S. citizen, my view of the world is much different from that of everyone whose parents were lucky enough not to have had the same unfortunate start in life that mine had endured. And, by the way, I will forever be grateful for how I was raised, as my parents instilled in me a sense of humanity, compassion, and an innate strength. A superpower, if you will, that has helped get me through my life's challenges, one day at a time.

The Trump administration had paved the way for Nazis to comfortably march with aplomb not only in the land of these God-forsaken bum fuck red states but also here in my LA backyard. They are zombies and seemingly everywhere, scenes from *The Night of the Living Dead*. Operative word: dead, especially if they intend to galvanize and resume the work of the Third Reich. As much as Trump wanted to be a mini-Hitler (well, surely not a mini, more of a big, fat, gross baboonish Hitler), there must be, at some point, a reckoning for his MAGA lunatic supporters. As long as I am breathing, or as God is my witness, there will be some kind of pushback from me. Let me put it this way: I won't be silent about this situation. It's been said that there are no coincidences, and this surely feels like it falls under that banner.

For context, my mother used to call me "an assimilated Jew"; that was her idea of a major insult. What I could never do was tell her why I had chosen a lifestyle that was so divorced from my religion or heritage. It wasn't shame that kept me from embracing Jewish culture—it was a childhood fear that the horror stories my mother told us about could somehow play out again. The terror of her experiences could reset and repeat in my life, like the automatic arm of a record player dropping the needle in an infinite loop. Watching in disgust as Trump supporters crept up from the hell holes they'd been hiding in, my fear was replaced with pride. I embraced my parents' legacy, my birthright, as an honor—and a responsibility. It is part of my story now, and I am obligated to carry it forward.

Unsurprisingly, this new global, socio-pathologically-politically-incorrect climate allowed White Nationalism and Neo-Nazism back onto the evening news and into the vernacular. When that blithering idiot talked about "Very fine people on both sides," it became clear that what loomed on the horizon for me was to become part of the much-needed counter-revolution against this indiscriminate, antise-mitic dog whistle, which somehow I could hear ringing in my ear like reveille, a clarion call to wake up and find a new path forward. It was my responsibility to do something that would matter to a swath of people affected by the cruelty of the gross baboon's words and what they implied.

After leaving Lily's employ and getting off opiates, I was able to land a producing gig from an old friend who had an agency that repre-sented fashion and beauty photographers. It was so weird returning to a work environment where the business wasn't conducted on a bed or while shopping for antiques and curiosities, as had become my norm. The desks at the new office were arranged (coincidentally like my sixth-grade class in Englewood Cliffs) in a square where people were forced to look at each other. Suddenly, I was transported back to that same feeling of helplessness and vulnerability I had experienced that April Fools' Day years ago when it was sink or swim. The advantage of this corporate combobulation was the massive Mac computers for us to hide behind to check personal emails, Instagram, and deciding what to have for lunch.

In short order, I was producing beauty shoots. I remembered that I'd mastered the art of being a highly functional, highly in demand, highly compensated drug addict that *The New York Times* called a "downtown Manhattan impresario" of all things. I could have been blindfolded for these kinds of projects and still come in on time and under budget.

I booked a two-day beauty shoot in NYC with a lifelong friend, Barrett, who was the client. She and I went way back. We had discov-ered partying as kids while attending the Young Judea after-school program at the Fort Lee Synagogue. We would sneak out, get high, and binge on White Castle hamburgers. Barrett and I reminisced about that time over fifty years ago when I pulled over and tried to kiss her and she slapped my face and said, "We'll park when I wanna park," which pretty much still sums her up today.

> SIDEBAR: There's an unwritten law in the glam business: the bigger the brand, the more self-aggrandized minions litter the set to feel validated for having otherwise thankless, menial cubicle jobs. At this particular gig, I stopped counting heads at forty.

Barrett knew all of my gritty details and was happy to book me for this gig. We talked about what it felt like to be single at the ripe old age of sixty, and the conversation soon led to the meaning of life, which I had no clue about. We enjoyed the superficial gossip spewed by the various teams: glam, stylist, black-clad publicists, and assorted nonsense. Barrett taught me the expression "resting bitch face," the perfect description of the look on most people's faces on set.

As I boarded the plane for my return flight to LA, I thought about something Barrett and I had started talking about that was gnawing at my soul. Not that there was anything wrong with being a lipstick whisperer, but really? Was this the meaning of life? What could I accomplish now that I had renewed my lease on it? I wanted to matter more than "job well done" coming in on or under budget for a product I didn't use nor care about. The person in the window seat was attractive, but I had no interest in striking up a conversation. He was nicely dressed, wore wire-rimmed glasses, and looked smart. I smiled, put my carry-on bag above the bulkhead, and settled into my Jet Blue polyester seat with my *Vanity Fair*, and as always, the change in cabin pressure had me helplessly falling into a deep sleep.

The plane's turbulence woke me, and I looked at the guy next to me, hoping that I hadn't snored. He was reading *Psychology Today*, and the cover story, "Life Lessons: Five Truths People Learn Too Late," was a punch in the gut. He noticed me ogling the cover, and I quipped, "That's painfully true," attempting a smile to cover the ache that I felt, wondering how many of those five lessons I had not yet learned. We chatted briefly about finding meaning and mattering. He wanted to become a therapist to help people, which was admirable. But when he asked me what I was doing, I could barely form the words. It wasn't an easy conversation to have because who was I helping? What was I doing besides simply surviving? How's that for bastardizing a term? Is simply surviving my own demons enough? I'm not sure; in fact, I'm positive that it is not. Something had to give.

On the Uber ride home, I resented that there was a cheap air freshener hanging from the rearview mirror AND it was raining. As we crawled up the 405, I stared out the window, pondering the meaning of life. Imagine suffering a dire existential crisis in a town not known for its depth. How could I live up to any expectations: my own, my family's, or those who found me hilarious? Was being the class clown my high point? That was a depressing thought. Maybe I could at least work toward finishing that book I started in Mexico so long ago. I felt hopeless.

The rain had stopped as I was about to get out of the car, which I took as a sign that good things were possible. I walked into the apartment, Woodstock and Alfie greeted me, and the frustration melted away. The dog sitter had left a sweet note saying that the kids were angels and if I needed her again, all I had to do was ask. I took the dogs for a walk, checked my iPhone, and noticed an email from the United States Holocaust Memorial Museum in Washington DC. Strange. I wasn't on the mailing list, and I scrolled down to see who it was from. What could the museum's musicologist want from me? As I read the email, I was so astonished that you could have knocked me over with a feather. I rushed back to my apartment to read it on my computer. The flabbergasting news was that the museum had confirmed that a piece of music written in the Klooga Concentration Camp in Estonia was being attributed to my uncle Wolf before the Nazis brutally murdered him on the eve of the liberation of the camp. He was only thirty years old. Operative word: flabbergasting!

> For decades, scholars wondered who wrote the song "Stay Silent" or how it sounded. Its true origins appeared in a book (White Nights and Black Days), a memoir that Mark Dvorzetsky, a doctor from Vilna, wrote about his time in Klooga. Another survivor, Raya Doron, transcribed the music and lyrics for the book. They were reminded of the song's meaning, written as a prayer of resistance, a silent act of defiance, which became a bond they shared in the darkest circumstances. The tune was composed by your uncle, Wolf Durmashkin, with words by poet Leyb Rosenthal. Neither man survived Klooga, but their song lives on to be re-imagined once more for a different moment in time.

I immediately called my sisters, who had also received the email. We talked for hours about our mom and how much she had revered her brother Wolf, who died so senselessly. It had been years since his name came up, since she had passed more than a decade ago. Throughout our childhood, the large black-and-white photograph of Wolf in a gilded frame had haunted my family as it hung in our dining room.

Wolf, 1914-1944

My mom spoke about Wolf as her greatest inspiration. He was a child prodigy who became the youngest conductor—and only Jew— of the Vilna Symphony Orchestra before World War II. When Mom's family was thrown into the ghetto, Wolf received a special dispensation to continue conducting the orchestra, yet he was forced to return to captivity nightly. In a heroic effort to keep hope and culture alive, Wolf and his fellow musicians created the Vilna Ghetto Orchestra by smuggling in every instrument—including a piano that they dismantled and then reassembled piece by piece. He also created a 100-voice choir that featured my mother. How unfortunate that she was no longer with us to appreciate this special acknowledgment of her beloved brother.

Vilna Ghetto Choir

After hanging up from the conversation with my sisters, I got into bed and started googling Wolf's name, but nothing came up. It was as though he never existed. A bolt of electricity shot through my soul—this was it. This was the sign I'd asked for. This was the opportunity that I'd been waiting for. This piece of unexpected history had risen from the ashes of the Holocaust. I had been given something to embrace, a noble gesture, and Wolf's message to carry forward. A ray of hope, as it had been for the prisoners and was now for me. Most importantly, it would be a way to honor my family and embrace the Jewish heritage I had shunned for decades.

Wolf Durmashkin with the Ghetto Symphonic Orchestra, Vilna Ghetto, September 5, 1942 (photo: Vilna Ghetto collection, the National Library of Israel).

Looking again at the email from the museum, I noticed the attachment, a screengrab of the page from Dr. Mark Dvorzetsky's memoir that consisted of scribbled-down musical notes accompanied by lyrics in another language. This was the proof of Wolf's existence and the provenance of his song. I desperately needed to hear the music and immediately forwarded it to my friend Guy, a pianist in Israel, asking him to record the notes on his iPhone and send it back to me.

My wake-up call to action from the ashes of the Holocaust

SO THAT HAPPENED

he next morning, I woke up with a gnawing ache in my heart, hoping it wasn't my father's angina and figuring instead that it was somewhat broken from the seismic boom that accompanied the discovery of this whisper from the ashes of the Holocaust. Until now, my uncle Wolf had been just one of the six million anonymous Jews who had perished from the Nazis' cruelty. Here was an opportunity to tell Wolf's story and give him a name, a face, and a legacy.

Legacy—now there's a loaded word that has haunted me for decades. Who gets to have one of those? When you stop to think of all the senseless killings in the concentration camps, who were these people? What were their hopes and dreams? Their lives were cut short, legacies lost, and it's impossible to imagine what could have been. Since I didn't love what the actual fuck my life was at the moment, I had to rethink my mission on Earth—correction—come up with one. If not for me, then for those who had never got their chance.

I dragged myself out of bed, made a pot of coffee, and sat at my large, black, French provincial desk that my mother would have loved. I had bought it on Craiglist, and the woman who sold it to me predicted it would "bring great fortune," as it had done for her. She was a real estate agent, and those people's idea of wealth didn't necessarily correlate with my perception of what makes someone wealthy. If money is the root of all evil and since I had none, did that make me a saint? I sipped my coffee and perused my usual morning news websites looking for what new shit storm Trump had kicked up overnight. Since the day that schmuck came bumbling down the escalator at Trump Tower debasing Mexicans, every day since then had been a journey to see how much lower into the depths of hell he would go. Today was no different, as the top story in *The New York Times* was "Trump's budget balloons deficit, cuts social safety net," a move that would reverberate for decades to come. All I wanted to know–was when the karma boomerang would do its thing and get this lowlife once and for all.

> SIDEBAR: Trump has been in my crosshairs since the 1980s when he helped usher in Yuppie culture. He was instrumental in destroying the gritty, sexier vibe of New York City alongside Nosferatu's twin brother, Rudy Giuliani, hence the nickname Ghouliani. They scrubbed the city of the grit that made it interesting. The newly pristine Times Square, coupled with the whole AIDS thing going on… well, let's just agree that the '80s sucked.

My heart skipped a beat when an email notification came from Guy, who had replied with an MP3 attachment. Excited, I listened to the haunting melody and teared up, moved by the notion that Wolf and his friend, Leyb, had created something beautiful and poetic during such a dark time. Just the thought of them sitting together in a cold, gray barrack, creating a song with a message of resisting their barbaric captors, was inconceivable. It's a testament to the indomitable human spirit and the power of art to help people transcend even the bleakest of circumstances.

The lyrics were in Yiddish, which is not my first nor a romance language. I had to start somewhere, and the first order of business was getting the lyrics translated into English. The extent of my Yiddish skills included a few insults and curse words befitting a Catskill Mountains refugee. I called Vivian, who knew some Yiddish, and she offered to reach out to a more prolific speaker of the language. Within minutes, the translated lyrics came through.

Let's be silent, let's be silent, and not a word be said.

With shuttered eyes, let's murmur a prayer.

Not the walls, nor the barbed wire, nor the guard who stands.

We can't let them take our tears.

No one can stop us from crying silently.

They can't steal our dignity.

There is one thing that is not prohibited to us—crying silently.

Seeing the translated lyrics, it felt like a remnant of a hymn, a mantra, an exhortation for Wolf's fellow prisoners, beseeching them to hold on tight to their dignity and not let these animals steal their humanity. Staying silent was a means of survival and a way to unite the prisoners in spiritual protest. They sang *Stay Silent* while doing hard labor, being starved and beaten. Tragically, in the end, Wolf, Leyb, and their comrades were senselessly burned alive on a pyre the day before the camp was liberated.

Attempting to visualize the unimaginable broke my heart. I played the music over and over. The more I heard it, the more certain I was that this was the only thing that mattered now. Wolf's perseverance and persistence while being persecuted were awe-inspiring. The song would serve as a talisman: a testament to survival—something my family and Jews in general are good at.

The Wolf experience erupted an energy force from deep down in my *genechtagazoink*. They say there are no coincidences. Therefore, the discovery of this song at this particular crossroads when I was open to receiving a truer, deeper connection to my family heritage was fortuitous. This feeling of reverence had eluded me for so many years. Suddenly and oddly, I thought of that horrific moment in the hospital, the night my father died, when Dr. Goldstein handed me my father's wedding ring and the anguish that I felt had set off a fit of rage that caused me to rip the glass charm off my neck and stomp on it. Damn, why didn't my father survive? That crushing blow had crippled my sense of self for so many years.

I chugged my third cup of coffee and started to make a plan.

Wolf was my God shot, and I'd be damned if I wouldn't do my damnedest to make him matter. Perhaps Wolf's song could be the brass ring that had always eluded me on the merry-go-round of life. Let's hope this real estate lady was prescient and Wolf's song was my good fortune. Now it was up to me to figure out what it could become—a performance, a new anthem against oppression, a play, a film. I knew it would honor my family in a way my mother would never have imagined.

SIDEBAR: Who am I kidding? My mom always hoped for this kind of recognition. In fact, I found a copy of a letter she sent to Otto Preminger suggesting he make a movie version of her life. She had written, "Your Highness, my life is a story of tremense proportions." (Not delirium tremens, she meant tremendous.) You gotta love her for that level of self-assuredness; naturally, she would have suggested that Sophia Loren play her in the movie.

With what I was beginning to visualize for this project, the title was troubling for me. Staying "silent" at this inflection point in our history with fascists at the gate would not do—not for me, nor for Wolf. I didn't think silence would suffice at a time when we needed to rally and speak up against an administration that felt more like an authoritarian regime. The Third Reich came to mind with every increasingly alarming news story out of Washington DC with that wanna-be fascist dictator spewing evil nonsense on a daily basis.

Who could I turn to as I ransacked what was left of my memory bank? Bingo! I reached out to Kara DioGuardi, a Grammy-nominated songwriter I'd worked with in the halcyon days of fashion. I shared the snippet of music from Guy, told her a little about Wolf, and asked if she would consider revising the lyrics to meet this moment. It was a time to come together, right now, and speak up against injustice, or rage against the machine. Something had to be done, and this was one thing I could contribute.

Within a few days, that angel, Kara, sent me her reinterpreted lyrics, and *Won't Be Silent*, inspired by Wolf, was born.

We won't be silent, won't be silent, not for one more day.
We'll speak out so future generations will be saved.
Won't close our eyes in fear and hide, we'll let our beauty reign.
Nothing stands between us and a world we dream to know.

We were made to love, no matter how much hate we face.
We will fight for those who cannot fight and need our strength.
Won't close our eyes in fear and hide, we'll let our beauty reign.
Nothing stands between us and a world we dream to know.

We'll break the silence, break the silence, screaming words of hope.

Won't be silent, won't be silent, not for one more day.
From now on we're healing from the truth in what we say.
We will fight for those who cannot fight and need our strength.
Nothing stands between us and a world we dream to know.

We'll break the silence, break the silence, screaming words of hope.
Won't be silent, won't be silent.

We'll break the silence, screaming words of hope.

Dear God,
Thank you.
Love,
ABE

With the wind in my sails, I called my friend Angelo D'Agostino, a music executive, and invited him and a couple of my closest friends, Stephen Galloway and Brian Wanee, to dinner. Not more than three sips into our drinks, I told them about this snippet of music discovered by the Holocaust Museum. As their jaws dropped, I told them the back story of my Uncle Wolf. We cried. Stephen wiped his tears and said, "Girl, you're like exhuming ashes of the Holocaust. Miss Thing, you gotta get this story out there." We laughed and continued crying. The encouraging takeaway was that Angelo, Stephen, and Brian are not Jewish, yet they were moved and heartened by Wolf's story. We talked about who would be the right artist to approach to record this song. A pop singer just wouldn't do. We needed to find someone with more gravitas who would deliver a heartfelt rendition worthy of Wolf.

Coincidentally, a long-time work associate was in LA. I had always adored working with Gayle, and when she asked what I was up to, I started to cry. After telling her the story, she said, "You have got to contact my friend who works with the Resistance Revival Chorus. They are amazing." I Googled immediately and read their mission statement:

> The Resistance Revival Chorus is a collective of Broadway performers, solo artists, gospel singers, and political activists. We believe that art and culture are essential to changing hearts, minds, and history; and we commit to the principle that joy is in itself an act of resistance.

The crying continued for several weeks, and it wasn't clear what I was crying about. A deep sadness, like mourning that I had expertly tucked away, had been unearthed from the depths of my psyche.

Something heavier was happening, and it would guide me through the process. Perhaps it was a collective guilt. As Lily used to say, "It's never one thing."

The concept for the *Won't Be Silent* project was evolving; what made the most sense was to draw a comparison between all marginalized groups who have suffered at the hands of extremists and oppression. It would be essential to tell Wolf's story in a way that had an optimistic message.

> Music as resistance has always been vital to those who've been oppressed; be it in the concentration camps, the cotton fields, or our inner-city streets. We sing about a better way of life because we know, universally, it can be.

The Resistance Revival Chorus were great messengers for the song, not only for their diversity but especially for how they banded together, having met at the Women's March in 2017 protesting the newly elected Trump administration. Serendipitous! I sent a weepy email, sharing how honored I would be for them to inaugurate Wolf's song. The logistics of getting twenty-five women together, coupled with my need to secure an angel investor, were daunting. Yet, by early June, we converged in a fabulous midtown Manhattan recording studio.

My friend Emanuel, an award-winning documentary filmmaker, captured the recording session, and an ad agency friend offered to put together a sizzle reel that I could use to pitch the project to studios and producers. Additionally, I had sharpened my "elevator pitch" down to eleven seconds:

> Can a song recently exhumed from the ashes of the Holocaust—written as a hymn of resistance to the Nazis—become a relevant anthem for social justice now?

During the rehearsal, the melodiousness of these goddesses singing in harmony catapulted the haunting, simple melody into the *We Shall Overcome* vibe we needed—then and now—at a time when everything seemed hopeless.

We kicked off the recording session with a kumbaya moment; the group held hands in a circle and shared a minute of silence for Wolf. I welcomed everyone in the studio—artists, friends, family, and Guy, who had flown in from Israel to accompany the Resistance Revival Chorus—with this statement:

> All of our ancestors have been oppressed somewhere
> along the line. We are all immigrants. So, this song is crucial
> because we can't and won't stay silent anymore. Not with
> the politics that are happening around the globe.

At the end of the recording session, the women wanted to bring *Won't Be Silent* and its message to the NYC streets. Their mantra is, "We want people in this current moment of resistance to use their voices." It's part of their magic and their DNA as a collective. Outside, we went to Fifth Avenue in midtown and attracted a group who applauded, and the reaction was just what I had hoped for. Wolf was on his way to mattering.

THERE'S NO BUSINESS LIKE
SHOAH BUSINESS

ere's a question I've never asked anyone before: Have you ever tried making a Holocaust movie? Lord knows there are several great ones: *Schindler's List, The Pianist,* and *Sophie's Choice,* to name a few. Yet, there are countless incredibly moving documentaries that barely see the light of day beyond the tight-knit community of Jews who have a direct connection or interest in the abomination that happened during World War II. Let's face it: the general population doesn't like being reminded of man's inhumanity to man. However, as the rise of fascist ideology creeps all around us, I, for one, have no tolerance for intolerance. Once again, we are at an inflection point where we must tell stories from the past in ways tht are palatable so future generations won't suffer the evil my parents did. Unfortunately, our society, with its current resistance to facing harsh realities, makes it harder for us to tell what happened unless we wrap everything with a pretty bow. We also crave immediate gratification, and stories of oppression sometimes lack appeal for people who have short attention spans.

When I decided to embark on this journey, I would never have expected such an uphill battle. In fact, once this *Wolf's Story* thing is said and done, I could conceivably make a film inspired by Mel Brooks' *The Producers,* only it would be about trying desperately to make a Holocaust movie in a town that is said to be run by Jews.

Wolf's heartbreaking story is so amazing and magical; who wouldn't want to help tell it? It's easier for the likes of George Clooney, Nicole Kidman, and that ilk to get moguls coughing up dough. But for everyone else, it is a Herculean task. Imagine trying to push a boulder up a steep hill, kind of like when the Jews were slaves in Egypt. Somehow, this far-reaching DNA prepared me for the next chapter of my life, which required a thick skin. If you can't laugh off being rejected umpteen times by agents, producers, directors, actors, and even social media influencers, then you need to get out of the game. I had mastered the art of taking rejection in my early days of being a short, fat Jew. That had taught me to laugh in the face of danger, even if crying was what felt appropriate. I even found a giggle at the high—and low—point when, yup, Steven Spielberg passed on the project. "Of course he did," I thought. Why should something that makes total sense make sense in Hollywood? It's all about Marvel superhero blockbusters, maybe the occasional chick flick, tons of reality shows, and countless limited series that no one is watching. Sadly, these producer types don't consider my crap to be crappy enough to produce. But did I fold up my cards and accept defeat? Have you met me?

That morning, I decided to go to Runyon Canyon, a breathtaking, arduous trail in the Hollywood Hills that everyone who was anyone might be seen hiking. Although it had been a long time since I climbed that mountain, I needed to feel the grounding that comes with the exertion and accomplishment of making it to the top, despite the occasional annoying selfie-taking influencer littering the joint. When you get to the peak, there is a bench that is my favorite place to sit and take in the view of the Hollywood sign on the left and the Pacific Ocean on the right. This spectacular vista always restores my sense of self and reminds me that anything is possible and how stunning LA is, from this distance, surely.

Jogging down the hill, I noticed a group of adorable Mexican teenagers giggling and having a grand old time. It was around the time when the big news story was the "Caravan of Migrants" moving towards the United States that Fox "News" (I use the term sarcastically) was trumping up (no pun intended) to scare people into voting for Republicans in the upcoming midterm election. These bright, smiling young people could conceivably be negatively impacted by the hysteria that the chief gross baboon was encouraging. I got into my car, where the normally soothing drone of the NPR newscasters' voices sounded unusually heightened. Stephen Miller, that wannabee SS Nazi Stormtrooper (though I considered him more of a Kapo), had implemented a cruel program that involved separating children from their parents at the U.S. border in Texas and putting immigrants in cages. CAGES!

SIDEBAR: What is a Kapo, a.k.a. Stephen Miller?
Kapos were Jewish concentration camp prisoners who worked with the Nazis as guards to carry out the will of the evil commandants, such as forcing their fellow Jews into the gas chambers and other horrendous acts. These pieces of shit were often as brutal as their SS counterparts.

Someone who was being interviewed on NPR sounded horrified at the family separation atrocity that was being implemented by Kapo Miller and said, "These kids are being put in concentration camps." That was the final straw. Hearing terms like *Nazis* and *concentration camps* was more than I could bear. Needing to release some steam, I booked a spin class at SoulCycle, so LA. When I arrived, something came over me and I started to tear up. As I was sitting on my bike minutes before class, the blonde woman beside me leaned in and asked, "Are you okay?" Naturally, I blurted out more than she had probably bargained for and told her about the kids, the cages, the Holocaust, *Won't Be Silent*, the urgency for the message to be translated into Spanish because of, well, everything. After class, she squeezed my arm and gave me the name and number of her friend Jaime Kohen, a Jewish, Mexican-Iranian, gay pop singer in Mexico City, so I could reach out to him about recording the song. Bingo.

"I will tell him to take your call," she offered.

This kicked off a series of events that I can only attribute to magical thinking. The creative producer part of my brain realized that everything having to do with Wolf's song should be filmed. Within a few weeks, I was in Mexico, where Jaime, Sandra, and Diego created a beautiful rendition of the song.

What happened next took the project in the direction I had intended from the get-go. The same angel investor, Jane, arranged a recording session for *Won't Be Silent* with a stunning R&B singer, Antonique Smith, whose voice is sheer magnificence. The opportunity to have a rendition that engaged the youth culture and embraced the initial concept, whether it's the concentration camps, the cotton fields, or inner-city streets, made perfect sense because music is the universal language we all share.

SIDEBAR: For fear of sounding like a jaded old queen, I just think there are angels on earth, and they were all showing up at that moment. Random people were coming together for this extraordinary storytelling extravaganza. You couldn't even make up something this fantastic; I can only tell this story because it happened, and it hasn't ended.

Antonique and her three fabulous producers took the music and mixed it into a high-spirited groove. It was a hallelujah-inducing boogie that Wolf might never have expected, but I trust he'd have appreciated it just the same.

Weeks later, at a book signing I attended in a private home, a 16-year-old girl played the violin as part of the evening's program. Moved, I asked her mother if her daughter would consider recording a version of Wolf's song. They were delighted, and as luck would have it, the mom was an accomplished pianist/songwriter and offered to accompany her daughter on the track. They invited me to their amazing home studio, where they recorded a hauntingly lovely rendition of the song that I particularly adore.

The most important conversation that needed to be filmed would take place when Kara DioGuardi and I discussed the song and Wolf. Fortunately, she was coming to LA the following week and offered her business partner's Hollywood Hills home with a magnificent panoramic view of the LA Basin as the setting. I wanted to get on film what had inspired her to create this masterpiece of meaning. It was important to hear her explanation: "Wolf wouldn't want us to say, 'Stay silent' now." We shared an extraordinary few hours talking, reminiscing, and recording the few bars of Wolf's original notes in her beautiful voice.

The ultimate miracle was an email from Mark Mast, conductor of the Bavarian Philharmonic Orchestra in Munich, Germany. I had met him the prior year and told him about finding Wolf's song and how, in a perfect world, it would be incredible to hear it played in Germany by an orchestra. Six months after that chance encounter, Mark told me to book a trip in March to experience what he had created based on our "perfect world" conversation. Mark had commissioned a young German composer, Tobias Forster, to expand Wolf's music into a full-length, spectacular score that would have made a Disney movie producer proud. The Spring Gala program at the magnificent Hercules Theater in Munich paid tribute to unfinished symphonies by great composers. The 56-piece orchestra played while the 82-member Bavarian Philharmonic Chorus sang the original hymn as written in Yiddish, followed by Tobias' stunning new, expanded orchestral interlude. The performance concluded with the chorus bellowing Kara's rendition of *Won't Be Silent*, sung with grit and intention, befitting a song of resistance.

Hearing Wolf's music presented alongside Schubert's Unfinished Symphony and Mozart's Unfinished Opera score was almost too much to take in; I had gotten Wolf Durmashkin the ultimate recognition that had been stolen from him. It was the acknowledgment for the ages. Wolf mattered; his work mattered. I bore witness to his legacy in this historic, landmark theater filled with 1,000 well-heeled Germans, where Adolf Hitler had seen countless performances during his reign. Decades after the Holocaust, what happened on March 17, 2019, was a kiss from heaven.

But it was what happened after the heart-wrenching performance that left me speechless. Me? Speechless? As I was standing in the lobby, an old, gray, hunched-over man approached me. He was crying and trembling and saying, "Es tut mir leid," which means "I'm sorry." He grabbed my shoulder and kept pleading for my forgiveness. I figured he must have felt guilty about something. He was the right age, surely. But having just experienced the ultimate musical healing moment, I didn't want anything to interfere with the divinity of this miraculous gift Mark had bestowed on me. Suddenly, the Craigslist lady who had sold me the desk came to mind. For me, these were the riches she predicted. We hear too often how money doesn't make people happy. In fact, isn't the expression "Money is the root of all evil"? All the gold in the world would not have made me feel any more joyful that day. It was all about Wolf; he would no longer be silenced.

Backstage, I was surrounded by the performers after this explosive, emotional evening. They had put their hearts and souls into the performance. These lovely, talented musicians and singers were grateful to be part of something so special. Then the first violinist, a handsome Aryan-looking young man, approached me with tears in his eyes and pulled me aside.

"I am thirty years old, and knowing our history, I have never been proud to say that I am German. I have felt such shame my whole life. But tonight, playing this music…in this place…I am proud to say I am German."

He leaned in, and we hugged and held on for an extra moment. We both felt a collective shift through this life-altering connectivity that neither of us had expected nor would ever forget.

The next morning, I woke up and wondered what the fuck had just happened. What I had experienced could never be accurately conveyed to my family, friends, or anyone, really. The atmosphere in the concert hall was electrifying. The response from everyone in the building was life-affirming. The feeling of accomplishment for giving Wolf a moment was immeasurable. I met Mark in the hotel lobby for coffee, and we savored the historic, wildly successful experience we had all shared. He leaned in and whispered, "That moment when Wolf wrote the melody, he was not a prisoner."

Emanuel, who had been filming all things *Won't Be Silent*, sent an email sharing his heartfelt appreciation:

> Sunday night's performance left a deep impression on me, my team, and my wife, who was in the audience. We are the descendants of the survivors, and the shadows of the Holocaust are with us still to this day, to be honest. Growing up as Jews in Munich is not a simple task and forces us to constantly reconsider and rethink our identity. Your efforts to make Wolf's music be finally recognized and performed publicly in Munich did a tremendous service to make us feel at home. This is not self-evident, and I thank you both from the bottom of my heart and Abe for allowing me to accompany him on his journey.

Just when I thought my heart couldn't break anymore, Tobias' reply arrived:

> Last year in April, our third child, beloved son Augustin, died at the age of two and a half after a necessary stem cell therapy and half a year in hospital. My family and I still have a hard time accepting our loss. We are amidst the process of slowly finding our way back to "regular life"…
>
> You can believe me, writing the composition also was an important aid for me to understand my pain and the pain of the Durmashkin family and of all the others who lost their lives so tragically.

On the plane ride home, I began to fully comprehend the profound impact this experience was having on me. The best unintended consequence was that Emanuel felt like the baby brother I had never had as we experienced such extraordinary moments together. The magnitude of exploding emotions he captured on film was like no other creative relationship I had ever had. We interviewed so many people to get their reactions, and each time, we looked at each other in awe of what we were involved with. Unfortunately, Emanuel wasn't there when I had that brief encounter with the old German man (a.k.a. definitely a former Nazi). The pain in his face spoke volumes, but what was so unforgettable was that I felt sorry for him at that moment. He had revealed without saying much that he needed to be forgiven.

The ability to forgive is what separates humans from animals. Don't get me wrong; plenty of humans are animals who lack the benevolence that completes their humanness. We see now how the dregs of society have been given a voice to spread their vomitous propaganda; worse yet, the deplorables they've elected are reveling in rolling back rights, marginalizing anyone they can, and marching in lockstep with their orange gross baboon wannabe-führer. Oh, and that certain pillow manufacturer.

The grace bestowed on those we forgive is a two-way street. In fact, when we forgive those who trespass upon us, it has to be without expectation of reciprocation. The act of forgiving in and of itself is grace. To expect forgiveness in return conflicts with why you are forgiving someone in the first place. It is not a cash-for-services deal. You forgive in order to clear a path forward to healing, to free your mind of negativity and resentment. To allow for better angels to guide you. To avoid the fucking karma boomerang that you hope gets whoever it is you are forgiving. (I didn't say I was perfect.)

Upon my return to Los Angeles, I couldn't help feeling alone, not lonely, because so many people had come into my life on this new journey where mattering had become my raison d'être. I was grateful that the pieces of this magnificent puzzle were coming together. Following my instincts is allowing me to pay homage to my uncle. Telling his untold story from the dark days of the Holocaust feels like a karmic gift. What happened in Munich in the shadows of where the Shoah happened is not lost on me. I was ready to sing, "There's no business like Shoah business."

WE CAN'T AND WON'T BE SILENT

'Twas NOT the night before Christmas when all through the house, not a creature was stirring, not even a…

Wait, in fact, it was 3:15 in the morning on March 20, 2020, after Governor Gavin Newsom implemented the COVID-19 lockdown. There was that same ominous feeling of "not a creature was stirring, not even a mouse." Actually, all of America wasn't stirring around that time, except for that heinous piece of shit Donald Trump tweaking and tweeting in the White House on his Adderall concoction, spewing nonsense about shoving bleach up someone's orifice as a possible remedy for the horrifying pandemic he had ushered into the United States due to his arrogance.

Within the next few days, the world became paralyzed in their homes, afraid to breathe for fear that the deadly virus was going to get us all. In one fell swoop, we held our collective breath, transfixed and terrorized as we were confronted with our mortality. No matter how much money you had, how evolved spiritually you thought you were, no matter what age you happened to be, death was knocking at your door. End times had come, and the only people who felt hopeful were Evangelical Christians because they could finally enjoy the rapture without having to schlep to Bethlehem.

Need I mention that the most contentious election of my lifetime, and yours, was underway? Democracy hung in the balance, and watching the motley crew doing their daily press briefing from the White House was like watching *A Nightmare on Elm Street* for the first time. It was the horror version of *Groundhog Day*, where nothing changed. Although, in our horror movie, things were getting progressively worse each day as people started dying in inconceivable numbers. Remember the refrigerator trucks? Talk about *The Invasion of the Body Snatchers*.

SIDEBAR: The goal is not for us to relive that nightmare. Just wanted to set the stage for you to fully comprehend the magnitude of realizing that at this point in my life, THIS had become my new reality, and the threat of losing the momentum of the *Won't Be Silent* project loomed larger than life itself.

So much had been accomplished in such a short period for the *Won't Be Silent* project that, sadly, I had to shut down the three outstanding performances I had arranged and booked for Wolf's song. With the help of the Transformative Justice Coalition, we were scheduled to travel in April to Charlotte, North Carolina, where the AME Church would have their gospel choir record a spirited rendition of the song. Yes, taking *Won't Be Silent* to church was so crucial for the moment because America was reeling from George Floyd's death, and Wolf's song could somehow be healing. From there, the plan was to head to Nashville for a country-inspired version to connect with our Southern brothers and sisters. The last shoot woud involve filming an East LA hip-hop version with teenage street dancers. Sadly, like so many other artists, I lost my funding, and there I was, home alone.

Coming to terms with the fact that all was lost in relation to my mission on Earth was a bitter pill to swallow. Then I heard about a social media app called TikTok where people were dancing. After watching for a few moments, I was glad that I had honed my dancing skills due to being a fat kid. (Remember "But he's a great dancer"?) So, my hubby and I threw on our kimonos, shimmied to Madonna, and got a lot of likes. We did a few other videos, always in our signature uniform, but, in hindsight, as much fun as it was, I felt foolish and too old. Something else was bubbling to the surface on TikTok that was far more interesting. People were talking honestly about their fears not only of the mass hysteria caused by the COVID-19 outbreak but also of the consequential election looming on the horizon. There was also a group of content creators who provided relevant, timely, and invaluable news and information that wasn't being covered by traditional media outlets because they were too busy obsessing on that heinous wildebeest in the White House.

My support for Joe Biden can be traced back to the moment he announced his candidacy for president, citing the best reason: a direct response to Trump's brazen, racist response to what had happened in

Charlottesville. Clearly, both of our lives had changed on that fateful and now grateful (for us) day. "Good people on both sides," my ass. This made me support Joe Biden unconditionally. Old, schmold, so am I. Especially compared to the self-aggrandizing, helicopter-parented Gen Z, whom the world was pinning too much hope on for them to register and show up to vote. Seeing how honest people were online about the catastrophe called Trump, I began pontificating about the administration, my support of Biden, and how happy I was that Joe had become the Democratic nominee. I would have been happier if Hillary had won in 2016, but I digress.

I went from 100 followers on TikTok to 4,000 overnight. But what felt right was engaging with faceless people who, like me, wanted to put an end to the Gross Baboon. Ideally, he would be Sirhan-Sirhaned, but voting him out was the legal best option. Within a week, I broke 10,000 constituents, as I prefer to call them because *followers* sounds too sycophanty-Christian-nationalisty for me.

Not since the early days of social media had I felt such an organic connection to nameless, faceless people, as weird as that sounds. We found each other and connected by watching each other's videos. I responded to people whose motives and desires to save our democracy became a rallying cry. My handle, @WontBeSilent, was the ideal title to embrace the new mission because what better way to say "I won't be silent" than by voting? Could it be that all the work on Wolf's song would have a fresh meaning, and this would be a revival of his message from the depths of despair to confront the currently looming Fourth Reich? Shifting gears to tackle the moment, I contacted the Voting Rights Alliance in DC. I offered to develop a series of public service announcements using the various versions of Wolf's song as the soundtrack to encourage young people of color to register and vote. In addition, the Spanish version we recorded in

Mexico City was used to promote Voto Latino, who wanted to engage their constituents with the No Guardaremos El Silencio message.

My hope was to inspire the next generation of new voters to understand that "your vote is your voice." You can't be silent in the face of an oppressive, ketchup-throwing, dictatorial, wanton, petulant buffoon like that thing that was stinking up the White House in 2020. It would be the year of infamy, not just one day, like America's D-Day or 9/11. (Not to mention my April Fool's Day, Ides of March, and testing positive. But I digress.) 2020 was a year full of those same raw emotions packed tight like sardines in cans, kinda like New Yorkers in a subway during rush hour. Breathing room, please.

The pro-democracy community was growing in leaps and bounds. The joy of seeing the music I had helped create be used in such a meaningful way at this inflection point was beyond rewarding. We may have been locked down due to COVID-19, but we were free to communicate through the magic of this newest, intoxicating media platform. If only my uncle and all those trapped in the horrors they suffered could have had a quadrillionth of a chance to be free. My dormant activist self was now fully engaged, and it was exhilarating to protest from the comfort of my Aeron chair. Call me a keyboard warrior if you dare. Still, I was fully immersed in getting people activated, not just pontificating like so many others, not to mention the Russian bot farms who were doing whatever they could to thwart our efforts by bombarding potential voters with misinformation.

We were no longer silenced, despite the millions of people who were homebound, whose jobs had been paused, and whose social lives had been cut short due to the pandemic. Doom and gloom bloomed, and we found refuge and connections through our iPhones. By June, this diverse community of democracy-obsessed Americans proved that we were going to use our verbal skill sets and galvanize our collective keyboard prowess coupled with our disdain for the orange Frankenstein. We planned to ruin the MAGA rally that he was holding in Tulsa, Oklahoma in June 2020 while the pandemic was still raging. Remember, it killed off Herman Cain simply by him attending the event. I'll never forget the look on Orange Goliath's face returning to DC after that rally when he knew in his cold, dead heart that he would lose the election. That long, lumbering walk off Marine One… we had never seen him looking so defeated, which was so encouraging for us. It was that night when the plans for January 6 began formulating. By the time the Biden-Trump debate happened in September, when Trump told his followers, "Stand back and stand by," it was all the proof I would need, in hindsight, to be certain that many of the elements of the MAGA insurrection had been set in motion.

The point is that we won. We fought to save our democracy in 2020 and took the Senate in January 2021 by ushering in a Jew and a Black man in the state of Georgia. Yes, I would love to take a bow and some credit for *Won't Be Silent* being a cog in the wheel of keeping America from fascism, one of my better accomplishments and a tribute to the joy of mattering. My *Won't Be Silent* project was a winner because Trump lost.

I can't focus on Americans who think white power is über alles, but I can continue to focus on what I can do that's positive and keep the message relevant as we navigate an uncertain future.

Most importantly, I get to tell the story of a man, my uncle, who never had his moment, and now he will get his uncollected legacy IF IT'S THE LAST THING I DO. The extraordinary *Won't Be Silent* community that has emerged through this project with its message of hope that rose from the ashes of the Holocaust will help build a brighter future so that another Holocaust won't happen. Despite this latest crop of misguided, propagandized, terrorist-loving, helicoptered, far-left, democracy-abandoning lemmings, and assorted Islamist antisemites threatening to wipe out the Jews, trust me, they will not win in the end.

> SIDEBAR: Let's face it: if Jews were meant to be wiped off the face of the Earth, we would not have survived forty years in the Sahara Desert after being slaves in Egypt building those fucking pyramids. The constipation from the matzoh alone would have taken us out.

YET, don't sit on your laurels, kids. Our work has just begun. The forces of evil that brought my grandparents to their violent, unfortunate deaths, coupled with what my parents had to endure, are not that far off on the horizon. If you squint hard enough, you can see the foreshadows of an America you won't recognize. Lord knows we already hear mumbling, rumbling, and the drumbeat of a new kind of war by evil factions here and abroad, which is why we can't, must not, and won't be silent.

DEFINITELY NOT THE END

IN MEMORIAM

TO MY REMARKABLE PARENTS,
HENNY AND SIMON

On the Cargo of Hope, 1949

It's been said that in matters of the heart, opposites attract. My parents' unlikely pairing proves that principle. They couldn't have been more different in their upbringing, personalities, and unfortunate experiences during the Holocaust. She, Dachau. He, Siberia. But thankfully, survivors they were.

When I discovered these rare photos years after my dad passed away, I was flabbergasted.

After surviving the gulags, my father joined the Resistance group Bricha (translation: Flight), which saved over 300,000 Holocaust survivors by leading them through the Austrian Alps and down the length of Italy to boats on the Mediterranean, waiting to shepherd them to freedom in Palestine.

Talk about super heroes.

Whereas immediately after the war, my mother and her sister Fanny who had miraculously survived Dachau together joined the Ex-Concentration Camp Orchestra. My mom became the soloist, while Fanny played the piano. They performed from 1945 to 1949 throughout Germany bringing music as a means of healing to the many Displaced Persons Camps.

The Ex-Concentration Camp Orchestra,
Nuremberg Opera House, May 1946

SIDEBAR: Now does everything make sense? With parents like that, you too would be cuckoo-laroo.

The most romantic memory of my parents is their storybook chance meeting on the *USS Greely* heading to America in 1949 on a journey to unknown fates and destinies. Having suffered through the war, all that mattered was a fresh start, a hopeful future.

On board the ship, which was nicknamed *Cargo of Hope*, they met at a dance. For my dad, it was love at first sight. He saw my mom sitting alone and asked her to dance. They spent the rest of the voyage learning about each other and discussing their plans for new lives in America. She wanted to become a singer, whereas he had a relative in the Midwest who had offered him a job and a place to stay.

From Milwaukee, for months, my dad wrote to my mom daily, expressing his love for her, but she wrote back that she wasn't sure when she could reciprocate. She was focused on taking singing lessons to restore the quality of her voice that had suffered as a result of malnutrition, starvation, and living in horrendous, cold circumstances at the hands of the Nazis as she was shuffled among several concentration camps.

My mom and her sister Fanny had miraculously survived Dachau together and emigrated to America. Fanny asked her if Simon was a good man, and Henny admitted, "He's more than good. He's a great man."

She realized how much she cared for him and agreed that they should be together. Simon happily came to New York, found a job, and they enjoyed a whirlwind romance and were married soon after.

My hope is to tell more of their stories. Stay tuned.

SIDEBAR: Not a day goes by that I don't think of them and thank God they were my teachers, my heroes, and my inspiration. They surely don't make them like they used to.

ACKNOWLEDGMENTS

"Frankly, Lizzie, I can't believe we're here." Lizzie Ciccone appeared like a mirage at a critical turning point when I could have easily put this book back on the To-Do Bucket List Shelf for another millennium. She charged in on a white horse and became my Winnie Cooper of wordsmithing. We laughed, we cried; it was definitely better than *Cats*.

To my fabulous family: Vivian Reisman & Rita Lerner and their kids, Jonathan & Anna, Sari & Ben, Jordana & Andy, Samantha & Andrew, David & Casey, Jason & Lauren and their kids, Eva, Grace, Judah, Kai-Wolf, Sierra, Leah, Isaac, Jacob, Ethan, Jordan, Joshua, Ella, Liam, & Chloe.

To Shlomi Barmi, my loving husband, for whom fate lent a hand and presented this beautiful, good-natured soul. Our chance union ultimately led to the space where I could write this book—and for that—I am eternally grateful. Not to mention that he loves to clean. You're the best.

Stephen Galloway, thank you for the endless laughter we have shared for over two decades. We met in Amsterdam during a blizzard over Christmas shortly after 9/11. A group of us were snowed in for days and watched every episode of *Absolutely Fabulous*, which is what Stephen is. Joy is at the heart of our friendship, and thankfully, he moved to Los Angeles, where we continue our tradition of giggling like school girls.

LeeAnne Stables—through our trials and tribulations, ups and downs, lovers, and other strangers—has been my rock and the matriarch of my chosen family.

Barrett Zinderman–my life-long, loyal, almost sister.

Angelo D'Agostino, Brain Wanee, and a few margaritas inspired the *Won't Be Silent* project. It was Angelo's creativity that paved the way, and I owe him a debt of gratitude into the afterlife.

Margaret Schell, Aeli Park, Zola Shulman, Michele Rosenthal, Cliff Salm, Scott Heller, Cindy Lee Rodgers, Dr. Carl Milner, Sonia Beker & Elyse Sholk, Lisa Pelto, Janet Tilden, Liz Omedes, Noel Berk, Audrey Nizen, Irene Dakota.

Johnna Escobedo Muscente, Chris Headley, Julian Kline, Clay Crider, Annie Washburn, Emily Giske, and the Fotzy Balloons.

In Memoriam: Donna Isman, Sal DeFalco, Carrie Fisher's spirit, and Estelle Branden, who got me back on my horse.

Wolf's Story documentary: Kara DioGuardi, Emanuel Rotstein, Guy Mintus, Aaron Zimmerman, Noelle Webb, Mark Mast, Tobias Forster, Bavarian Symphony and Chorus, Jaime Kohen, Sandra Lau, Diego Rojas, Daniela Suarez, Antonique Smith, Darryl Farmer, Suburban Plaza, Otto Arsenault, Daniele De Vuono, Resistance Revival Chorus, Isolde Fair, and Starr Parodi, Fran & Steve Berman, Karla Schönebeck, and Justin Jones. To Jane Oster Sinisi for making it all possible. I will forever be grateful.

Won't Be Silent documentary: Selena Gomez, Stacey Abrams, David Seidler, Clara Hendon, Kent Kubena, Angus Wall, Piper Gates and the Makemake Entertainment Crew, Kristi Jacobson, Orly Ravid–Creative Arts Legal LLP.

The 6 Million Jews
The People of Israel

Our Democracy, if we can keep it.
My awesome Political TikTok Community

Thank you for making me look so cool, Art Director, Marc Balet, Photographers, Diana Gomez and Rankin.